TEACHING OF PHYSICS

R.K. Shrivastava

Saurabh
Publishing House
4263/3, Ansari Road,
Darya Ganj, New Delhi-110002

Published by:

SAURABH PUBLISHING HOUSE

Distributed by:

LOTUS PRESS

4263/3, Ansari Road, Darya Ganj, New Delhi-110002

Ph: 32903912, 23280047 • E-mail: lotus_press@sify.com

Saurabh Publishing is an imprint of

Lotus Press

Teaching of Physics

ISBN : 978-81-89005-50-4 (H/B)

Printed in India by Anand Sons, Delhi

Preface

Physics is a natural science that involves the study of matter and its motion through space time, as well as all applicable concepts, including energy and force. More broadly, it is the general analysis of nature, conducted in order to understand how the universe behaves.

Physics is one of the oldest academic disciplines, perhaps the oldest through its inclusion of astronomy. Over the last two millennia, physics had been considered synonymous with philosophy, chemistry, and certain branches of mathematics and biology, but during the Scientific Revolution in the 16th century, it emerged to become a unique modern science in its own right. However, in some subject areas such as in mathematical physics and quantum chemistry, the boundaries of physics remain difficult to distinguish.

Physics is both significant and influential, in part because advances in its understanding have often translated into new technologies, but also because new ideas in physics often resonate with other sciences, mathematics, and philosophy. For example, advances in the understanding of electromagnetism or nuclear physics led directly to the development of new products which have dramatically transformed modern-day society, such as television, computers, domestic appliances, and nuclear weapons; advances in thermodynamics led to the development of motorized transport; and advances in mechanics inspired the development of calculus.

Theorists seek to develop mathematical models that both agree with existing experiments and successfully predict future results, while experimentalists devise and perform experiments to test theoretical predictions and explore new phenomena. Although theory and experiment are developed separately, they are strongly dependent upon each other. Progress in physics frequently comes about when experimentalists make a discovery that existing theories cannot explain, or when new theories generate experimentally testable predictions, which inspire new experiments.

Theoretical physics has historically taken inspiration from philosophy; electromagnetism was unified this way. Beyond the known universe, the field of theoretical physics also deals with hypothetical issues, such as parallel universes, a multiverse, and higher dimensions.

Experimental physics informs, and is informed by, engineering and technology. Experimental physicists involved in basic research design and perform experiments with equipment such as particle accelerators and lasers, whereas those involved in applied research often work in industry, developing technologies such as magnetic resonance imaging (MRI) and transistors. Feynman has noted that experimentalists may seek areas which are not well explored by theorists.

The knowledge of physics is essential, for every body, because of its immense value in our every day life. Physics teaching-learning process provides the scientists, Researchers and Students a better platform for learning the physics.

This book is an invaluable resource for teaching introductory physics, from high school to calculus-based college courses, this instructional tool presents systematic observations based upon research into how physics students come to learn and understand physics.

R.K. Shrivastava

Contents

1

Teaching of Physics: Methods, Tools and Techniques

Definition and Meaning

Physics is a natural science that involves the study of matter and its motion through space time, as well as all applicable concepts, including energy and force. More broadly, it is the general analysis of nature, conducted in order to understand how the universe behaves.

Physics is one of the oldest academic disciplines, perhaps the oldest through its inclusion of astronomy. Over the last two millennia, physics had been considered synonymous with philosophy, chemistry, and certain branches of mathematics and biology, but during the Scientific Revolution in the 16th century, it emerged to become a unique modern science in its own right. However, in some subject areas such as in mathematical physics and quantum chemistry, the boundaries of physics remain difficult to distinguish.

Physics is both significant and influential, in part because advances in its understanding have often translated into new technologies, but also because new ideas in physics often resonate with other sciences, mathematics, and philosophy. For example, advances in the understanding of electromagnetism or nuclear physics led directly to the development of new products which have dramatically transformed modern-day society, such as television, computers, domestic appliances, and nuclear weapons; advances in thermodynamics led to the development of motorized transport; and advances in mechanics inspired the development of calculus.

Scope and Aims

Physics covers a wide range of phenomena, from elementary particles (such as quarks, neutrinos and electrons) to the largest superclusters of galaxies. Included in these phenomena are the most basic objects from which all other things are composed, and therefore physics is sometimes called the "fundamental science". Physics aims to describe the various phenomenon that occur in nature in terms of simpler phenomena. Thus, physics aims to both connect the things observable to humans to root causes, and then to try to connect these causes together.

For example, the ancient Chinese observed that certain rocks (lodestone) were attracted to one another by some invisible force. This effect was later called magnetism, and was first rigorously studied in the 17th century. A little earlier than the Chinese, the ancient Greeks knew of other objects such as amber, that when rubbed with fur would cause a similar invisible attraction between the two. This was also first studied rigorously in the 17th century, and came to be called electricity. Thus, physics had come to understand two observations of nature in terms of some root cause (electricity and magnetism). However, further work in the 19th century revealed that these two forces were just two different aspects of one force – electromagnetism.

This process of "unifying" forces continues today, and electromagnetism and the weak nuclear force are now considered to be two aspects of the electroweak interaction.

The Scientific Method

Physicists use the scientific method to test the validity of a physical theory, using a methodical approach to compare the implications of the theory in question with the associated conclusions drawn from experiments and observations conducted to test it. Experiments and observations are to be collected and matched with the predictions and hypotheses made by a theory, thus aiding in the determination or the validity/invalidity of the theory.

Theories which are very well supported by data and have never failed any competent empirical test are often called scientific laws, or natural laws. Of course, all theories, including those called scientific laws, can always be replaced by more accurate, generalized statements if a disagreement of theory with observed data is ever found.

Theory and Experiment

Theorists seek to develop mathematical models that both agree with existing experiments and successfully predict future results, while experimentalists devise and perform experiments to test theoretical predictions and explore new phenomena. Although theory and experiment are developed separately, they are strongly dependent upon each other. Progress in physics frequently comes about when experimentalists make a discovery that existing theories cannot explain, or when new theories generate experimentally testable predictions, which inspire new experiments.

Physicists who work at the interplay of theory and experiment are called phenomenologists. Phenomenologists look at the complex phenomena observed in experiment and work to relate them to fundamental theory.

Theoretical physics has historically taken inspiration from philosophy; electromagnetism was unified this way. Beyond the known universe, the field of theoretical physics also deals with hypothetical issues, such as parallel universes, a multiverse, and higher dimensions. Theorists invoke these ideas in hopes of solving particular problems with existing theories. They then explore the consequences of these ideas and work toward making testable predictions.

Experimental physics informs, and is informed by, engineering and technology. Experimental physicists involved in basic research design and perform experiments with equipment such as particle accelerators and lasers, whereas those involved in applied research often work in industry, developing technologies such as Magnetic Resonance Imaging (MRI) and transistors. Feynman has noted that experimentalists may seek areas which are not well explored by theorists.

Relation to Mathematics and the Other Sciences

In the *Assayer* (1622), Galileo noted that mathematics is the language in which Nature expresses its laws. Most experimental results in physics are numerical measurements, and theories in physics use mathematics to give numerical results to match these measurements.

Physics relies upon mathematics to provide the logical framework in which physical laws may be precisely formulated and predictions quantified. Whenever analytic solutions of equations are not feasible, numerical analysis and simulations may be utilized. Thus, scientific computation is an integral part of physics, and the field of computational physics is an active area of research.

A key difference between physics and mathematics is that since physics is ultimately concerned with descriptions of the material world, it tests its theories by comparing the predictions of its theories with data procured from observations and experimentation, whereas mathematics is concerned with abstract patterns, not limited by those observed in the real world. The distinction, however, is not always clear-cut. There is a large area of research intermediate between physics and mathematics, known as mathematical physics.

Physics is also intimately related to many other sciences, as well as applied fields like engineering and medicine. The principles of physics find applications throughout the other natural sciences as some phenomena studied in physics, such as the conservation of energy, are common to *all* material systems. Other phenomena, such as superconductivity, stem from these laws, but are not laws themselves because they only appear in some systems.

Physics is often said to be the "fundamental science" (chemistry is sometimes included), because each of the other disciplines (biology, chemistry, geology, material science, engineering, medicine etc.) deals with particular types of material systems that obey the laws of physics. For example, chemistry is the science of collections of matter (such as gases and liquids formed of atoms and molecules) and the processes known as chemical reactions that result in the change of chemical substances.

The structure, reactivity, and properties of a chemical compound are determined by the properties of the underlying molecules, which may be well-described by areas of physics such as quantum mechanics, or quantum chemistry, thermodynamics, and electromagnetism.

Philosophical implications

Physics in many ways stems from ancient Greek philosophy. From Thales' first attempt to characterize matter, to Democritus' deduction that matter ought to reduce to an invariant state, the Ptolemaic astronomy of a crystalline firmament, and Aristotle's book *Physics*, different Greek philosophers advanced their own theories of nature. Well into the 18th century, physics was known as natural philosophy.

By the 19th century physics was realized as a positive science and a distinct discipline separate from philosophy and the other sciences. Physics, as with the rest of science, relies on philosophy of science to give an adequate description of the scientific method. The scientific method employs a priori reasoning as well as a posteriori reasoning and the use of Bayesian inference to measure the validity of a given theory.

The development of physics has answered many questions of early philosophers, but has also raised new questions. Study of the philosophical issues surrounding physics, the philosophy of physics, involves issues such as the nature of space and time, determinism, and metaphysical outlooks such as empiricism, naturalism and realism.

Many physicists have written about the philosophical implications of their work, for instance Laplace, who championed causal determinism, and Erwin Schrodinger, who wrote on quantum mechanics. The mathematical physicist Roger Penrose has been called a Platonist by Stephen Hawking, a view Penrose discusses in his book, *The Road to Reality*. Hawking refers to himself as an "unashamed reductionist" and takes issue with Penrose's views.

History

Since antiquity, people have tried to understand the behaviour of the natural world. One great mystery was the predictable behaviour of celestial objects such as the Sun and the Moon. Several theories were proposed, the majority of which were disproved.

The philosopher Thales (ca. 624–546 BC) first refused to accept various supernatural, religious or mythological explanations for natural phenomena, proclaiming that every event had a natural cause. Early physical theories were largely couched in philosophical terms, and never verified by systematic experimental testing as is popular today. Many of the commonly accepted works of Ptolemy and Aristotle are not always found to match everyday observations.

Even so, many ancient philosophers and astronomers gave correct descriptions in atomism and astronomy. Leucippus (first half of 5th century BC) first proposed atomism, while Archimedes derived many correct quantitative descriptions of mechanics, statics and hydrostatics, including an explanation for the principle of the lever. The Middle Ages saw the emergence of an experimental physics taking shape among medieval Muslim physicists, the most famous being Alhazen, followed by modern physics largely taking shape among early modern European physicists, the most famous being Isaac Newton, who built on the works of Galileo Galilei and Johannes Kepler. In the 20th century, the work of Albert Einstein marked a new direction in physics that continues to the present day.

Core Theories

While physics deals with a wide variety of systems, certain theories are used by all physicists. Each of these theories were experimentally tested numerous times and found correct as an approximation of nature (within a certain domain of validity). For instance, the theory of classical mechanics accurately describes the motion of objects, provided they are much larger than atoms and moving at much less than the speed of light. These theories continue to be areas of active research, and a remarkable aspect of classical mechanics known as chaos was discovered in the 20th century, three centuries after the original formulation of classical mechanics by Isaac Newton.

These central theories are important tools for research into more specialized topics, and any physicist, regardless of his or her specialization, is expected to be literate in them. These include classical mechanics, quantum mechanics, thermodynamics and statistical mechanics, electromagnetism, and special relativity.

Research Fields

Contemporary research in physics can be broadly divided into condensed matter physics; atomic, molecular, and optical physics; particle physics; astrophysics; geophysics and biophysics. Some physics departments also support research in Physics education.

Since the twentieth century, the individual fields of physics have become increasingly specialized, and today most physicists work in a single field for their entire careers. "Universalists" such as Albert Einstein (1879–1955) and Lev Landau (1908–1968), who worked in multiple fields of physics, are now very rare.

Condensed Matter

Velocity-distribution data of a gas of rubidium atoms, confirming the discovery of a new phase of matter, the Bose–Einstein condensate

Condensed matter physics is the field of physics that deals with the macroscopic physical properties of matter. In particular, it is concerned with the "condensed" phases that appear whenever the number of constituents in a system is extremely large and the interactions between the constituents are strong.

The most familiar examples of condensed phases are solids and liquids, which arise from the bonding and electromagnetic force between atoms. More exotic condensed phases include the superfluid and the Bose–Einstein condensate found in certain atomic systems at very low temperature, the superconducting phase exhibited by conduction electrons in certain materials, and the and antiferromagnetic phases of spins on atomic lattices.

Table 1.1. Major fields of physics, along with their subfields and the theories they employ

Field	Subfields	Major theories	Concepts
Astrophysics	Astronomy, Astrometry, Cosmology, Gravitation physics, High-energy astrophysics, Planetary astrophysics, Plasma physics, Solar Physics, Space physics, Stellar astrophysics	Big Bang, Cosmic inflation, General relativity, Newton's law of universal gravitation, Lambda-CDM model, Magneto hydrodynamics	Black hole, Cosmic background radiation, Cosmic string, Cosmos, Dark energy, Dark matter, Galaxy, Gravity, Gravitational radiation, Gravitational singularity, Planet, Solar system, Star, Supernova, Universe
Atomic, molecular, and optical physics	Atomic physics, Molecular physics, Atomic and Molecular astrophysics, Chemical physics, Optics, Photonics	Quantum optics, Quantum chemistry, Quantum information science	Photon, Atom, Molecule, Diffraction, Electromagnetic radiation, Laser, Polarization (waves), Spectral line, Casimir effect
Particle physics	Nuclear physics, Nuclear astrophysics, Particle astrophysics, Particle physics phenomenology	Standard Model, Quantum field theory, Quantum electrodynamics, Quantum chromodynamics, Electroweak theory, Effective field theory, Lattice field theory, Lattice gauge theory, Gauge theory, Supersymmetry, Grand unification theory, Superstring theory, M-theory	Fundamental force (gravitational, electromagnetic, weak, strong), Elementary particle, Spin, Antimatter, Spontaneous symmetry breaking, Neutrino oscillation, Seesaw mechanism, Brane, String, Quantum gravity, Theory of everything, Vacuum energy
Condensed matter physics	Solid state physics, High pressure physics, Low-temperature physics, Surface Physics, Nanoscale and Mesoscopic physics, Polymer physics	BCS theory, Bloch wave, Density functional theory, Fermi gas, Fermi liquid, Many-body theory, Statistical Mechanics	Phases (gas, liquid, solid), Bose-Einstein condensate, Electrical conduction, Phonon, Magnetism, Self-organization, Semiconductor, superconductor, superfluid, Spin

Condensed matter physics is by far the largest field of contemporary physics. Historically, condensed matter physics grew out of solid-state physics, which is now considered one of its main subfields. The term *Condensed Matter Physics* was apparently coined by Philip Anderson when he renamed his research group previously *solid-state theory* in 1967.

In 1978, the Division of Solid State Physics at the American Physical Society was renamed as the Division of Condensed Matter Physics. Condensed matter physics has a large overlap with chemistry, materials science, nanotechnology and engineering.

Atomic, Molecular and Optical Physics

Atomic, molecular, and optical physics (AMO) is the study of matter-matter and light-matter interactions on the scale of single atoms or structures containing a few atoms. The three areas are grouped together because of their interrelationships, the similarity of methods used, and the commonality of the energy scales that are relevant. All three areas include both classical and quantum treatments; they can treat their subject from a microscopic view.

Atomic physics studies the electron shells of atoms. Current research focuses on activities in quantum control, cooling and trapping of atoms and ions, low-temperature collision dynamics, the collective behaviour of atoms in weakly interacting gases (Bose–Einstein Condensates and dilute Fermi degenerate systems), precision measurements of fundamental constants, and the effects of electron correlation on structure and dynamics. Atomic physics is influenced by the nucleus (see, e.g., hyperfine splitting), but intra-nuclear phenomenon such as fission and fusion are considered part of high energy physics.

Molecular physics focuses on multi-atomic structures and their internal and external interactions with matter and light. Optical physics is distinct from optics in that it tends to focus not on the control of classical light fields by macroscopic objects, but on the fundamental properties of optical fields and their interactions with matter in the microscopic realm.

High Energy / Particle Physics

A simulated event in the CMS detector of the Large Hadron Collider, featuring a possible appearance of the Higgs boson.

Particle physics is the study of the elementary constituents of matter and energy, and the interactions between them. It may also be called "high energy physics", because many elementary particles do not occur naturally, but are created only during high energy collisions of other particles, as can be detected in particle accelerators.

Currently, the interactions of elementary particles are described by the Standard Model. The model accounts for the 12 known particles of matter (quarks and leptons) that interact *via* the strong, weak, and electromagnetic fundamental forces. Dynamics are described in terms of matter particles exchanging force carrier particles (gluons, W and Z bosons, and photons, respectively). The Standard Model also predicts a particle known as the Higgs boson, the existence of which has not yet been verified; as of 2010, searches for it are underway in the Tevatron at Fermilab and in the Large Hadron Collider at CERN.

Astrophysics

The deepest visible-light image of the universe, the Hubble Ultra Deep Field Astrophysics and astronomy are the application of the theories and methods of physics to the study of stellar structure, stellar evolution, the origin of the solar system, and related problems of cosmology. Because astrophysics is a broad subject, astrophysicists typically apply many disciplines of physics, including mechanics, electromagnetism, statistical mechanics, thermodynamics, quantum mechanics, relativity, nuclear and particle physics, and atomic and molecular physics.

The discovery by Karl Jansky in 1931 that radio signals were emitted by celestial bodies initiated the science of radio astronomy. Most recently, the frontiers of astronomy have been expanded by space exploration. Perturbations and interference from the earth's atmosphere make space-based observations necessary for infrared, ultraviolet, gamma-ray, and X-ray astronomy.

Physical cosmology is the study of the formation and evolution of the universe on its largest scales. Albert Einstein's theory of relativity plays a central role in all modern cosmological theories. In the early 20th century, Hubble's discovery that the universe was expanding, as shown by the Hubble diagram, prompted rival explanations known as the steady state universe and the Big Bang.

The Big Bang was confirmed by the success of Big Bang nucleosynthesis and the discovery of the cosmic microwave background in 1964. The Big Bang model rests on two theoretical pillars: Albert Einstein's general relativity and the cosmological principle. Cosmologists have recently established the ËCDM model of the evolution of the universe, which includes cosmic inflation, dark energy and dark matter.

Numerous possibilities and discoveries are anticipated to emerge from new data from the Fermi Gamma-ray Space Telescope over the upcoming decade and vastly revise or clarify existing models of the Universe. In particular, the potential for a tremendous discovery surrounding dark matter is possible over the next several years. Fermi will search for evidence that dark matter is composed of weakly interacting massive particles, complementing similar experiments with the Large Hadron Collider and other underground detectors.

IBEX is already yielding new astrophysical discoveries: "No one knows what is creating the ENA (energetic neutral atoms) ribbon" along the termination shock of the solar wind, "but everyone agrees that it means the textbook picture of the heliosphere in which the solar system's enveloping pocket filled with the solar wind's charged particles is plowing through the onrushing 'galactic wind' of the interstellar medium in the shape of a comet is wrong."

Fundamental Physics

While physics aims to discover universal laws, its theories lie in explicit domains of applicability. Loosely speaking, the laws of classical physics accurately describe systems whose important length scales are greater than the atomic scale and whose motions are much slower than the speed of light. Outside of this domain, observations do not match their predictions. Albert Einstein contributed the framework of special relativity, which replaced notions of absolute time and space with spacetime and allowed an accurate description of systems whose components have speeds approaching the speed of light. Max Planck, Erwin Schrodinger, and others introduced quantum mechanics, a probabilistic notion of particles and interactions that allowed an accurate description of atomic and subatomic scales. Later, quantum field theory unified quantum mechanics and special relativity. General relativity allowed for a dynamical, curved spacetime, with which highly massive systems and the large-scale structure of the universe can be well described. General relativity has not yet been unified with the other fundamental descriptions; several candidates theories of quantum gravity are being developed.

Application and Influence

Applied physics is a general term for physics research which is intended for a particular use. An applied physics curriculum usually contains a few classes in an applied discipline, like geology or electrical engineering. It usually differs from engineering in that an applied physicist may not be designing something in particular, but rather is using physics or conducting physics research with the aim of developing new technologies or solving a problem.

The approach is similar to that of applied mathematics. Applied physicists can also be interested in the use of physics for scientific research. For instance, people working on accelerator physics might seek to build better particle detectors for research in theoretical physics.

Physics is used heavily in engineering. For example, Statics, a subfield of mechanics, is used in the building of bridges and other structures. The understanding and use of acoustics results in better concert halls; similarly, the use of optics creates better optical devices. An understanding of physics makes for more realistic flight simulators, video games, and movies, and is often critical in forensic investigations.

With the standard consensus that the laws of physics are universal and do not change with time, physics can be used to study things that would ordinarily be mired in uncertainty. For example, in the study of the origin of the Earth, one can reasonably model Earth's mass, temperature, and rate of rotation, over time. It also allows for simulations in engineering which drastically speed up the development of a new technology.

But there is also considerable interdisciplinarity in the physicist's methods, and so many other important fields are influenced by physics: e.g. presently the fields of econophysics plays an important role, as well as sociophysics.

Current Research

A typical event described by physics: a magnet levitating above a superconductor demonstrates the Meissner effect.

Research in physics is continually progressing on a large number of fronts. In condensed matter physics, an important unsolved theoretical problem is that of high-temperature superconductivity. Many condensed matter experiments are aiming to fabricate workable spintronics and quantum computers.

In particle physics, the first pieces of experimental evidence for physics beyond the Standard Model have begun to appear. Foremost among these are indications that neutrinos have non-zero mass. These experimental results appear to have solved the long-standing solar neutrino problem, and the physics of massive neutrinos remains an area of active theoretical and experimental research. Particle accelerators have begun probing energy scales in the TeV range, in which experimentalists are hoping to find evidence for the Higgs boson and supersymmetric particles.

Theoretical attempts to unify quantum mechanics and general relativity into a single theory of quantum gravity, a programme ongoing for over half a century, have not yet been decisively resolved. The current leading candidates are M-theory, superstring theory and loop quantum gravity.

Many astronomical and cosmological phenomena have yet to be satisfactorily explained, including the existence of ultra-high energy cosmic rays, the baryon asymmetry, the acceleration of the universe and the anomalous rotation rates of galaxies.

Although much progress has been made in high-energy, quantum, and astronomical physics, many everyday phenomena involving complexity, chaos, or turbulence are still poorly understood. Complex problems that seem like they could be solved by a clever application of dynamics and mechanics remain unsolved; examples include the formation of sandpiles, nodes in trickling water, the shape of water droplets, mechanisms of surface tension catastrophes, and self-sorting in shaken heterogeneous collections.

❑❑❑

2

World of Instrumental Laws

Introduction

It is convenient that Russell talks about physics, and that the laws he praises are its fundamental equations—Hamilton's equations or Schroedinger's, or the equations of general relativity. That is what I want to discuss too. But I hold just the reverse of Russell's view. I am in favour of causes and opposed to laws. I think that, given the way modern theories of mathematical physics work, it makes sense only to believe their causal claims and not their explanatory laws.

1. Explaining By Causes

We know that there are various things one can be doing in explaining. Two are of importance here: in explaining a phenomenon one can cite the causes of that phenomenon; or one can set the phenomenon in a general theoretical framework. The framework of modern physics is mathematical, and good explanations will generally allow us to make quite precise calculations about the phenomena we explain. Rene Thom remarks the difference between these two kinds of explanation, though he thinks that only the causes really explain: Descartes with his vertices, his hooked atoms, and the like explained everything and calculated nothing; Newton, with the inverse square of gravitation, calculated everything and explained nothing'.

Unlike Thom, to call both explanation, so long as we do not illicitly attribute to theoretical explanation features that apply only to causal explanation. There is a tradition, since the time of Aristotle, of deliberately conflating the two. But we will argue that they function quite differently in modern physics. If we accept Descartes's causal story as adequate, we must count his claims about hooked atoms and vortices true. But we do not use Newton's inverse square law as if it were either true or false.

One powerful argument speaks against our claim and for the truth of explanatory laws the argument from coincidence. Those who take laws seriously tend to subscribe to what Gilbert Harman has called inference to the best explanation. They assume that the fact that a law explains provides evidence that the law is true. The more diverse the phenomena that it explains, the more likely it is to be true. It would be an absurd coincidence if a wide variety of different kinds of phenomena were all explained by a particular law, and yet were not in reality consequent from the law. Thus the argument from coincidence supports a good many of the inferences we make to best explanations.

The method of inference to the best explanation is subject to an important constraint, however—the requirement of non-redundancy. We can infer the truth of an explanation only if there are no alternatives that account in an equally satisfactory way for the phenomena. In physics nowadays, I shall argue, an acceptable causal story is supposed to satisfy this requirement. But exactly the opposite is the case with the specific equations and models that make up our theoretical explanations. There is redundancy of theoretical treatment, but not of causal account.

There is, we think, a simple reason for this: causes make their effects happen. We begin with a phenomenon which, relative to our other general beliefs, we think would not occur unless something peculiar brought it about. In physics we often mark this belief by labelling the phenomena as effects—the Sorbet effect, the Zeeman effect, the Hall effect. An effect needs something to bring it about, and the peculiar features of the effect depend on the particular nature of the cause, so that in so far as we think we have got it right we are entitled to infer the character of the cause from the character of the effect.

But equations do not bring about the phenomenological laws we derive from them (even if the phenomenological laws are themselves equations). Nor are they used in physics as if they did. The specific equations we use to treat particular phenomena provide a way of casting the phenomena into the general framework of the theory. Thus we are able to treat a variety of disparate phenomena in a similar way, and to make use of the theory to make quite precise calculations. For both of these purposes it is an advantage to multiply theoretical treatments.

Pierre Duhem used the redundancy requirement as an argument against scientific realism, and recently Hilary Putman uses it as an argument against realism in general. Both propose that, in principle, for any explanation of any amount of data there will always be an equally satisfactory alternative. The history of science suggests that this claim may be right: we constantly construct better explanations to replace those of the past. But such arguments are irrelevant here; they do not distinguish between causal claims and theoretical accounts. Both are likely to be replaced by better accounts in the future.

We will use two examples to show this. The first—quantum damping and its associated line broadening—is a phenomenon whose understanding is critical to the theory of lasers. Here we have a single causal story, but a fruitful multiplication of successful theoretical accounts. This contrasts with the unacceptable multiplication of causal stories in the second example.

There is one question we should consider before looking at the examples, a question pressed by two colleagues in philosophy of science, Dan Hausman and Robert Ennis. How are we to distinguish the explanatory laws, which we argue are not to be taken literally, from the causal claims and more pedestrian statements of fact, which are? The short answer is that there is no way. A typical way of treating a problem like this is to find some independent criterion—ideally syntactical, but more realistically semantical hich will divide the claims of a theory into two parts. Then it is argued that claims of one kind are to be taken literally, whereas those of the other kind function in some different way.

This is not what we have in mind. We think of a physics theory as providing an explanatory scheme into which phenomena of interest can be fitted. We agree with Duhem here. The scheme simplifies and organizes the phenomena so that we can treat similarly happenings that are phenomenologically different, and differently ones that are phenomenologically the same. It is part of the nature of this organizing activity that it cannot be done very well if we stick too closely to stating what is true. Some claims of the theory must be literally descriptive if the theory is to be brought to bear on the phenomena; but we suspect that there is no general independent way of characterizing which these will be. What is important to realize is that if the theory is to have considerable explanatory power, most of its fundamental claims will not state truths, and that this will in general include the bulk of our most highly prized laws and equations.

2. Examples: Quantum Damping

In radiative damping, atoms de-excite, giving off photons whose frequencies depend on the energy levels of the atom.

We know by experiment that the emission line observed in a spectroscope for a radiating atom is not infinitely sharp, but rather has a finite linewidth; that is, there is a spread of frequencies in the light emitted. What causes this natural linewidth? Here is the standard answer which physicists give, quoted from a good textbook on quantum radiation theory by William Louisell:

> There are many interactions which may broaden an atomic line, but the most fundamental one is the reaction of the radiation field on the atom. That is, when an atom decays spontaneously from an excited state radiatively, it emits a quantum of energy into the radiation field. This radiation may be reabsorbed by the atom. The reaction of the field on the atom gives the atom a linewidth and causes the original level to be shifted as we show. This is the source of the natural linewidth and the Lamb shift.

Following his mathematical treatment of the radiative decay, Louisell continues:

> We see that the atom is continually emitting and reabsorbing quanta of radiation. The energy level shift does not require energy to be conserved while the damping requires energy conservation. Thus damping is brought about by the emission and absorption of real photons while the photons emitted and absorbed which contribute to the energy shift are called virtual photons.

This account is universally agreed upon. Damping, and its associated line broadening, are brought about by the emission and absorption of real photons.

Here we have a causal story; but not a mathematical treatment. We have not yet set line broadening into the general mathematical framework of quantum mechanics. There are many ways to do this. One of the Springer Tracts by G.S. Agarwal summarizes the basic treatments which are offered. He lists six different approaches in his table of contents: (1) Weisskopf-Wigner method; (2) Heitler-Ma method; (3) Goldberger-Watson method; (4) Quantum

Statistical method: master equations; (5) Langevin equations corresponding to the master equation and a c-number representation; and (6) neoclassical theory of spontaneous emission.

Before going on to discuss these six approaches, we will give one other example. The theory of damping forms the core of current quantum treatments of lasers. Figure 2.1 on next page is a diagram from a summary article by H. Haken on 'the' quantum theory of the laser. We see that the situation I described for damping theory is even worse here. There are so many different treatments that Haken provides a 'family tree' to set straight their connections. Looking at the situation Haken himself describes it as a case of 'theory overkill'. Laser theory is an extreme case, but I think there is no doubt that this kind of redundancy of treatment, which Haken and Agarwal picture, is common throughout physics.

Agarwal describes six treatments of line broadening. All six provide precise and accurate calculations for the shape and width of the broadened line. How do they differ? All of the approaches employ the basic format of quantum mechanics. Each writes down a Schroedinger equation; but it is a different equation in each different treatment. (Actually among the six treatments there are really just three different equations.) The view that we are attacking takes theoretical explanations to provide, as best they can, statements of objective laws. On this view the six approaches that Agarwal lists compete with one another; they offer different laws for exactly the same phenomena.

But this is not Agarwal's attitude. Different approaches are useful for different purposes; they complement rather than compete. The Langevin and Master equations of (4) and (5), for instance, have forms borrowed from statistical mechanics. They were introduced in part because the development of lasers created an interest in photon correlation experiments. Clearly, if we have statistical questions, it is a good idea to start with the kind of equations from which we know how to get statistical answers.

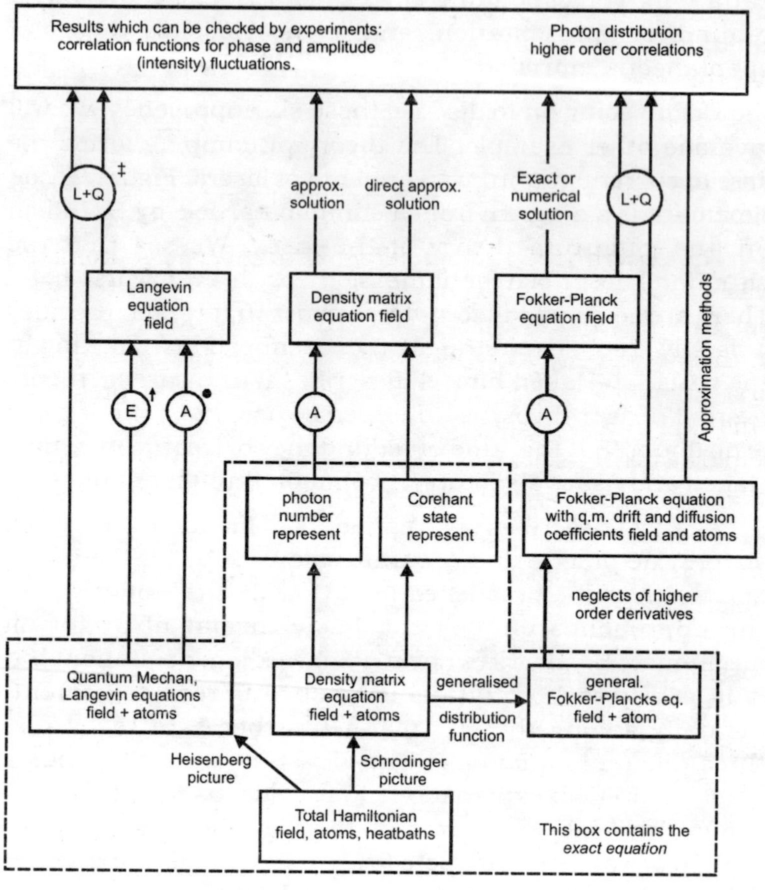

Figure. 2.1. Family tree of the quantum theory of the laser.

Let us consider an objection to the point of view I have been urging. We all know that physicists write down the kinds of equations they know how to solve; if they cannot use one approximation, they try another; and when they find a technique that works, they apply it in any place they can. These are commonplace observations that remind us of the pragmatic attitude of physicists. Perhaps, contrary to my argument, the multiplication of theoretical treatments says more about this pragmatic orientation than it does about how explanatory laws ought to be viewed. We disagree. We think that it does speak about laws, and in particular shows how laws differ from causes. We do not have the same pragmatic tolerance of causal alternatives. We do not use first one causal story in explanation, then another, depending on the ease of calculation, or whatever.

The case of the radiometer illustrates. The radiometer was introduced by William Crookes in 1873, but it is still not clear what makes it work. Recall from the Introduction to these essays that there are three plausible theories. The first attributes the motion of the vanes to light pressure. This explanation is now universally rejected. As M. Goldman remarks in "The Radiometer Revisited".

A simple calculation shows that on a typical British summer day, when the sky is a uniform grey (equally luminous all over) the torque from the black and silver faces exactly balance, so that for a perfect radiometer [i.e., a radiometer with a perfect vacuum] no motion would be possible.

Two explanations still contend. The first is the more standard, textbook account, which is supported by Goldman's calculations. It supposes that the motion is caused by the perpendicular pressure of the gas in the perfect vacuum against the vanes. But as we have seen, on Maxwell's account the motion must be due to the tangential stress created by the gas slipping around the edge of the vanes. There is a sense in which Maxwell and Goldman may both be right: the motion may be caused by a combination of tangential and perpendicular stress. But this is not what they claim. Each claims that the factor he cites is the single significant factor in bringing about the motion, and only one or the other of these claims can be accepted. This situation clearly constrasts with Agarwal's different theoretical treatments. In so far as we are interested in giving a causal explanation of the motion, we must settle on one account or the other. We cannot use first one account, then the other, according to our convenience.

We know of this example through Francis Everitt, who thinks of building an experiment that would resolve the question. We mention Everitt's experiment again because it argues for the difference in objectivity which we urge between theoretical laws and causal claims. It reminds us that unlike theoretical accounts, which can be justified only by an inference to the best explanation, causal accounts have an independent test of their truth: we can perform controlled experiments to find out if our causal stories are right or wrong. Experiments of these kinds in fact play an important role in an example from which Wesley Salmon defends inferences to the best explanation.

3. The Argument From Coincidence

In a recent paper Salmon considers Jean Perrin's arguments for the existence of atoms and for the truth of Avagadro's hypothesis that there are a fixed number of molecules in any gram mole of a fluid. Perrin performed meticulous experiments on Brownian motion in colloids from which he was able to calculate Avagadro's number quite precisely. His 1913 tract, in which he summarizes his experiments and recounts the evidence for the existence of atoms, helped sway the community of physicists in favour of these hypotheses. Besides Brownian motion, Perrin lists thirteen quite different physical situations which yield a determination of Avogadro's number. So much evidence of such a variety of kinds all pointing to the same value must surely convince us, urges Perrin, that atoms exist and that Avogadro's hypothesis is true.

For many, Perrin's reasoning is a paradigm of inference to the best explanation; and it shows the soundness of that method. We think this misdiagnoses the structure of the argument. Perrin does not make an inference to the best explanation, where explanation includes anything from theoretical laws to a detailed description of how the explanandum was brought about. He makes rather a more restricted inference an inference to the most probable cause.

A well-designed experiment is constructed to allow us to infer the character of the cause from the character of its more readily observable effects. Prior to Perrin, chemists focused their attention on the size and velocities of the suspended particles. But this study was unrewarding; the measurements were difficult and the results did not signify much. Perrin instead studied the height distribution of the Brownian granules at equilibrium. From his results, with a relatively simple model for the collision interactions, he was able to calculate Avogadro's number. Perrin was a brilliant experimenter. It was part of his genius that he was able to find quite specific effects which were peculiarly sensitive to the exact character of the causes he wanted to study. Given his model, the fact that the carrier fluids had just 6×10^{23} atoms for every mole made precise and calculable differences to the distribution he observed.

The role of the model is important. It brings out exactly what part coincidence plays in the structure of Perrin's argument. Our reasoning from the character of the effect to the character of the cause is always against a background of other knowledge. We aim to find out about a cause with a particular structure. What effects appear as a result of that structure will be highly sensitive to the exact nature of the causal processes which connect the two. If we are mistaken about the processes that link cause and effect in our experiment, what we observe may not result in the way we think from the cause under study. Our results may be a mere artefact of the experiment, and our conclusions will be worthless.

Perrin explicitly has this worry about the first of the thirteen phenomena he cites: the viscosity of gases, which yields a value for Avogadro's number via Van der Waal's equation and the kinetic theory of gases. In his *Atoms* he writes that 'the probable error, for all these numbers is roughly 30 per cent, owing to the approximations made in the calculations that lead to the Clausius-Maxwell and Van der Waal's equations.' He continues: 'The Kinetic Theory justly excites our admiration. [But] it fails to carry complete conviction, because of the many hypotheses it involves. What sets Perrin's worries to rest? He tell us himself in the next sentence: 'If by entirely independent routes we are led to the same values for the molecular magnitudes, we shall certainly find our faith in the theory considerably strengthened.'

Here is where coincidence enters. We have thirteen phenomena from which we can calculate Avogadro's number. Any one of these phenomena if we were sure enough about the details of how the atomic behavour gives rise to it would be good enough to convince us that Avogadro is right. Frequently we are not sure enough; we want further assurance that we are observing genuine results and not experimental artefacts. This is the case with Perrin. He lacks confidence in some of the models on which his calculations are based. But he can appeal to coincidence. Would it not be a coincidence if each of the observations was an artefact, and yet all agreed so closely about Avogadro's number?

The convergence of results provides reason for thinking that the various models used in Perrin's diverse calculations were each good enough. It thus reassures us that those models can legitimately be used to infer the nature of the cause from the character of the effects.

In each of Perrin's thirteen cases we infer a concrete cause from a concrete effect. We are entitled to do so because we assume that causes make effects occur in just the way that they do, via specific, concrete causal processes. The structure of the cause physically determines the structure of the effect. Coincidence enters Perrin's argument, but not in a way that supports inference to the best explanation in general. There is no connection analogous to causal propagation between theoretical laws and the phenomenological generalizations which they bring together and explain. Explanatory laws summarize phenomenological laws; they do not make them true. Coincidence will not help with laws. We have no ground for inferring from any phenomenological law that an explanatory law must be just so; multiplying cases cannot help.

We mentioned that Gilbert Harman introduced the expression 'inference to the best explanation'. Harman uses two examples in his original paper. The first is the example that we have just been discussing: coming to believe in atoms. The second is a common and important kind of example from everyday life: inferring that the butler did it. Notice that these are both cases in which we infer facts about concrete causes: they are not inferences to the laws of some general explanatory scheme. Like Perrin's argument, these do not vindicate a general method for inferring the truth of explanatory laws. What they illustrate is a far more restrictive kind of inference: inference to the best cause.

Conclusion

Perrin did not make an inference to the best explanation, only an inference to the most probable cause. This is typical of modern physics. 'Competing' theoretical treatments treatment that write down different laws for the same phenomena are encouraged in physics, but only a single causal story is allowed. Although philosophers generally believe in laws and deny causes, explanatory practice in physics is just the reverse.

❑❑❑

3

Phenomenological Laws in Physics

Introduction

Suppose that some fundamental laws are used to explain a phenomenological law. The ultra-realist thinks that the phenomenological law is true because of the more fundamental laws. One elementary account of this is that the fundamental laws make the phenomenological laws true. The truth of the phenomenological laws derives from the truth of the fundamental laws in a quite literal sense-something like a causal relation exists between them. This is the view of the seventeenth-century mechanical philosophy of Robert Boyle and Robert Hooke. When God wrote the Book of Nature, he inscribed the fundamental laws of mechanics and he laid down the initial distribution of matter in the universe. Whatever phenomenological laws would be true fell out as a consequence. But this is not only the view of the seventeenth-century mechanical philosophy. It is a view that lies at the heart of a lot of current-day philosophy of science—particularly certain kinds of reductionism and I think it is in part responsible for the widespread appeal of the deductive-nomological model of explanation, though certainly it is not a view that the original proponents of the D-N model, such as Hempel, and Grunbaum, and Nagel, would ever have considered. We used to hold something like this view myself, and we used it in my classes to help students adopt the D-N model. We tried to explain the view with two stories of creation.

Imagine that God is about to write the Book of Nature with Saint Peter as his assistant. He might proceed in the way that the mechanical philosophy supposed. He himself decided what the fundamental laws of mechanics were to be and how matter was to be distributed in space. Then he left to Saint Peter the laborious but unimaginative task of calculating what phenomenological laws would evolve in such a universe. This is a story that gives content to the reductionist view that the laws of mechanics are fundamental and all the rest are epi-phenomenal.

On the other hand, God may have had a special concern for what regularities would obtain in nature. There were to be no distinctions among laws: God himself would dictate each and every one of them—not only the laws of mechanics, but also the laws of chemical bonding, of cell physiology, of small group interactions, and so on. In this second story Saint Peter's task is far more demanding. To Saint Peter was left the difficult and delicate job of finding some possible arrangement of matter at the start that would allow all the different laws to work together throughout history without inconsistency. On this account all the laws are true at once, and none are more fundamental than the rest.

The different roles of God and Saint Peter are essential here: they make sense of the idea that, among a whole collection of laws every one of which is supposed to be true, some are more basic or more true than others. For the 17th century mechanical philosophy, God and the Book of Nature were legitimate devices for thinking of laws and the relations among them. But for most of us nowadays these stories are mere metaphors. For a long time we used the metaphors, and hunted for some non-metaphorical analyses. I now think that it cannot be done. Without God and the Book of Nature there is no sense to be made of the idea that one law derives from another in nature, that the fundamental laws are basic and that the others hold literally 'on account of' the fundamental ones.

Here the D-N model of explanation might seem to help. In order to explain and defend our reductionist views, we look for some quasi-causal relations among laws in nature. When we fail to find any reasonable way to characterize these relations in nature, we transfer our attention to language. The deductive relations that are supposed to hold between the laws of a scientific explanation act as a formal-mode stand-in for the causal relations we fail to find in the material world. But the D-N model itself is no argument for realism once we have stripped away the questionable metaphysics. So long as we think that deductive relations among statements of law mirror the order of responsibility among the laws themselves, we can see why explanatory success should argue for the truth of the explaining laws. Without the metaphysics, the fact that a handful of elegant equations can organize a lot of complex information about a host of phenomenological laws is no argument for the truth of those equations. We need some story about what the connection between the fundamental equations and the more complicated laws is supposed to be. There we saw that Adolf Grunbaum has outlined such a story. His outline I think coincides with the views of many contemporary realists. Grunbaum's view eschews metaphysics and should be acceptable to any modern empiricist. Recall that Grunbaum says:

> It is crucial to realize that while (a more comprehensive law) *G* entails (a less comprehensive law) *L* logically, thereby providing an explanation of *L*, *G* is not the 'cause' of *L*. More specifically, laws are explained not by showing the regularities they affirm to be products of the operation of causes but rather by recognizing their truth to be special cases of more comprehensive truths.

We call this kind of account of the relationship between fundamental and phenomenological laws a generic-specific account. It holds that in any particular set of circumstances the fundamental explanatory laws and the phenomenological laws that they explain both make the same claims. Phenomenological laws are what the fundamental laws amount to in the circumstances at hand. But the fundamental laws are superior because they state the facts in a more general way so as to make claims about a variety of different circumstances as well.

The generic-specific account is nicely supported by the deductive-nomological model of explanation: when fundamental laws explain a phenomenological law, the phenomenological law is deduced from the more fundamental in conjunction with a description of the circumstances in which the phenomenological law obtains. The deduction shows just what claims the fundamental laws make in the circumstances described.

But explanations are seldom in fact deductive, so the generic-specific account gains little support from actual explanatory practice. Wesley Salmon and Richard Jeffrey and now many others, have argued persuasively that explanations are not arguments. But their views seem to bear most directly on the explanations of single events; and many philosophers still expect that the kind of explanations that we are concerned with here, where one law is derived from others more fundamental, will still follow the D-N form. One reason that the D-N account often seems adequate for these cases is that it starts looking at explanations only after a lot of scientific work has already been done. It ignores the fact that explanations in physics generally begin with a model. The calculation of the small signals properties of amplifiers, which we discuss in the next section, is an example. We first decide which model to use—perhaps the T-model, perhaps the hybrid-Π model. Only then can we write down the equations with which we will begin our derivation.

Which model is the right one? Each has certain advantages and disadvantages. The T-model approach to calculating the midband properties of the CE stage is direct and simple, but if we need to know how the CE stage changes when the bias conditions change, we would need to know how all the parameters in the transistor circuit vary with bias. It is incredibly difficult to produce these results in a T-model. The T-model also lacks generality, for it requires a new analysis for each change in configuration, whereas the hybrid-Π model approach is most useful in the systematic analysis of networks. This is generally the situation when we have to bring theory to bear on a real physical system like an amplifier. For different purposes, different models with different incompatible laws are best, and there is no single model which just suits the circumstances. The facts of the situation do not pick out one right model to use.

Here we want to lay aside my worries about models, and think about how derivations proceed once a model has been chosen. Proponents of the D-N view tend to think that at least then the generic-specific account holds good. But this view is patently mistaken when one looks at real derivations in physics or engineering. It is never strict deduction that takes you from the fundamental equations at the beginning to the phenomenological laws at the end. Instead we require a variety of different approximations. In any field of physics there are at most a handful of rigorous solutions, and those usually for highly artificial situations. Engineering is worse.

Proponents of the generic-specific account are apt to think that the use of approximations is no real objection to their view. They have a story to tell about approximations: the process of deriving an approximate solution parallels a D-N explanation. One begins with some general equations which we hold to be exact, and a description of the situation to which they apply. Often it is difficult, if not impossible, to solve these equations rigorously, so we rely on our description of the situation to suggest approximating procedures.

In these cases the approximate solution is just a stand-in. We suppose that the rigorous solution gives the better results; but because of the calculational difficulties, we must satisfy ourselves with some approximation to it.

Sometimes this story is not far off. Approximations occasionally work just like this. Consider, for example, the equation used to determine the equivalent air speed, V_E, of a plane (where P_T is total pressure, P_o is ambient pressure, ñs is sea level density, and M is a Mach number):

$$V_E = \left[2\left(\frac{P_T - P_0}{\rho s}\right)\times\left(\frac{1}{1+M^2/4+M^4/40}\right)\right]^{\frac{1}{2}} \qquad \text{...(3.1)}$$

The value for V_E determined by this equation is close to the plane's true speed.

Approximations occur in connection with (3.1) in two distinct but typical ways. First, the second term,

$$\frac{1}{1+M^2/4+M^4/40}$$

is significant only as the speed of the plane approaches Mach One. If $M < 0.5$, the second term is discarded because the result for V_E given by

$$2\left(\frac{P_T - P_0}{\rho s}\right)$$

will differ insignificantly from the result given by (3.1). Given this insignificant variation, we can approximate V_E by using

$$V_E = \left[2\left(\frac{P_T - P_0}{\rho s}\right)\right]^{\frac{1}{2}} \qquad \text{...(3.2)}$$

for $M < 0.5$. Secondly, (3.1) is already an approximation, and not an exact equation. The term

$$\frac{1}{1 + M^2/4 + M^4/40}$$

has other terms in the denominator. It is a Taylor series expansion. The next term in the expansion is M6/1600, so we get

$$\frac{1}{1 + M^2/4 + M^4/40 + M^6/1600}$$

in the denominator, and so on. For Mach numbers less than one, the error that results from ignoring this third term is less than one per cent, so we truncate and use only two terms.

Why does the plane travel with a velocity, V, roughly equal to

$$\left[2\left(\frac{P_T - P_0}{\rho s}\right)\right]^{\frac{1}{2}}$$

Because of equation (3.1). In fact the plane is really travelling at a speed equal to

$$\left[2\left(\frac{P_T - P_0}{\rho s}\right) \times \frac{1}{1 + M^2/4 + M^4/40 + \ldots}\right]^{\frac{1}{2}}.$$

But since M is less than 0.5, we do not notice the difference. Here the derivation of the plane's speed parallels a covering law account. We assume that equation (3.1) is a true law that covers the situation the plane is in. Each step away from equation (3.1) takes us a little further from the true speed. But each step we take is justified by the facts of the case, and if we are careful, we will not go too far wrong. The final result will be close enough to the true answer.

This is a neat picture, but it is not all that typical. Most cases abound with problems for the generic-specific account. Two seem to me especially damaging: (1) practical approximations usually improve on the accuracy of our fundamental laws. Generally, the doctored results are far more accurate than the rigorous outcomes which are strictly implied by the laws with which we begin. (2) On the generic-specific account the steps of the derivation are supposed to show how the fundamental laws make the same claims as the phenomenological laws, given the facts of the situation. But seldom are the facts enough to justify the derivation. Where approximations are called for, even a complete knowledge of the circumstances may not provide the additional premises necessary to deduce the phenomenological laws from the fundamental equations that explain them. Choices must be made which are not dictated by the facts.

We have already knows that this is so with the choice of models. But it is also the case with approximation procedures: the choice is constrained, but not dictated by the facts, and different choices give rise to different, incompatible results. The generic-specific account fails because the content of the phenomenological laws we derive is not contained in the fundamental laws which explain them.

1. Approximations that Improve on Laws

On the generic-specific account, any approximation detracts from truth. But it is hard to find examples of this at the level where approximations connect theory with reality, and that is where the generic-specific account must work if it is to ensure that the fundamental laws are true in the real world. Generally, at this level approximations take us away from theory and each step away from theory moves closer towards the truth. This illustrate with two examples with the help of Jon Nordby.

1.1. An Amplifier Model

Consider an amplifier constructed according to Figure 3.1. There are two ways to calculate the small signal properties of this amplifier, the T-model and the hybrid-Π model. The first substitutes a circuit model for the transistor and analyses the resulting network. The second characterizes the transistor as a set of two-port parameters and calculates the small signal properties of the amplifier in terms of these parameters. The two models are shown in Figures 3.2 and 3.3 inside the dotted area.

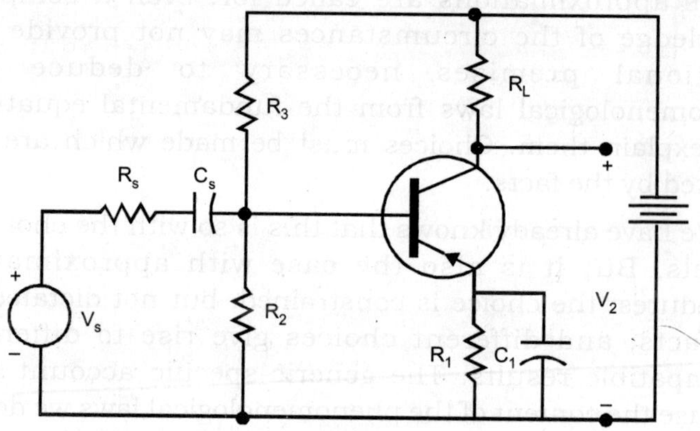

Figure. 3.1

The application of these transistor models in specific situations gives a first rough approximation of transistor parameters at low frequencies. These parameters can be theoretically estimated without having to make any measurements on the actual circuit. But the theoretical estimates are often grossly inaccurate due to specific causal features present in the actual circuit, but missing from the models.

One can imagine handling this problem by constructing a larger, more complex model that includes the missing causal features. But such a model would have to be highly specific to the circuit in question and would thus have no general applicability.

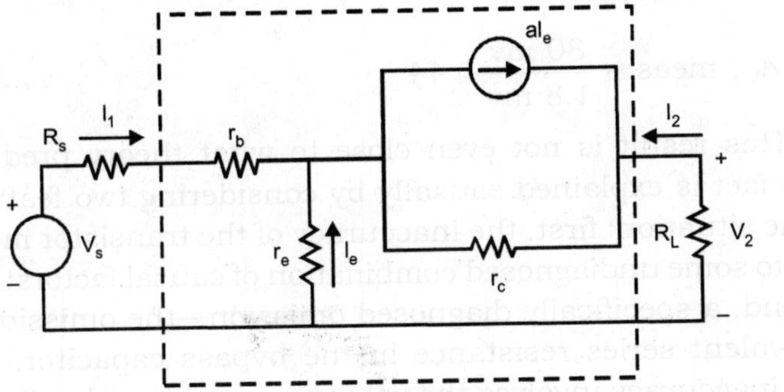

Figure. 3.2

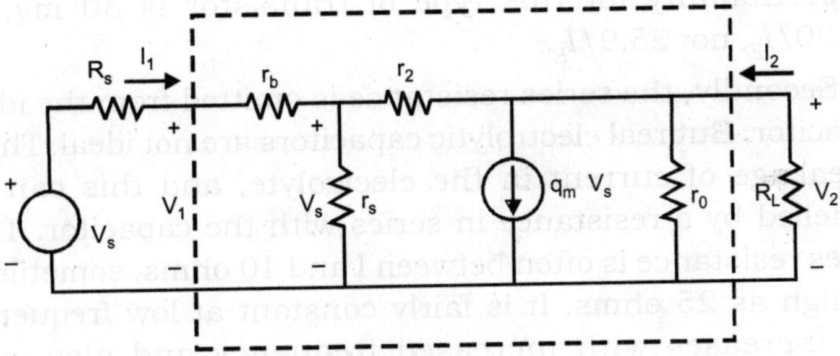

Figure. 3.3

Instead a different procedure is followed. Measurements of the relevant parameters are made on the actual circuit under study, and then the measured values rather than the theoretically predicted values are used for further calculations in the original models. To illustrate, consider an actual amplifier, built and tested such that I_E = 1 ma; R_L = 2.7 * 15 = 2.3 k ohm; R_1 = 1 k ohm. ß = 162 and R_S– 1 k ohm and assume r_b = 50 ohms. The theoretical expectation of midband gain is

$$|A_V| = \frac{R_L}{r_e + (r_b + R_S)(1-\alpha)} = \frac{2.3 \text{ k ohms}}{32 \text{ k ohms}} = 72 \qquad \text{...(3.3)}$$

The actual measured midband gain for this amplifier with an output voltage at $f = 2$ kHz and source voltage at 1.8 mv and 2 kHz, is

$$A_V, \text{ meas} = \frac{80 \text{ mv}}{1.8 \text{ mv}} = 44 \quad \text{...(3.4)}$$

This result is not even close to what theory predicts. This fact is explained causally by considering two features of the situation: first, the inaccuracy of the transistor model due to some undiagnosed combination of causal factors; and second, a specifically diagnosed omission—the omission of equivalent series resistance in the bypass capacitor. The first inaccuracy involves the value assigned to re by theory. In theory, $r_e = kT/qI_E$, which is approximately $25.9/I_E$. The actual measurements indicate that the constant of proportionality for this type of transistor is 30 mv, so $r_e = 30/I_E$, not $25.9/I_E$.

Secondly, the series resistance is omitted from the ideal capacitor. But real electrolytic capacitors are not ideal. There is leakage of current in the electrolyte, and this can be modelled by a resistance in series with the capacitor. This series resistance is often between I and 10 ohms, sometimes as high as 25 ohms. It is fairly constant at low frequency but increases with increased frequency and also with increased temperature. In this specific case, the series resistance, is measured as 12 ohms.

r_{c_1}

We must now modify (3.3) to account for these features, given our measured result in (3.4) of A_V, meas. = 44:

$$|A_V| = \frac{R_L}{r_e + (r_b + R_S)(1-\alpha) + r_{c_1}} \quad \text{...(3.5)}$$

Solving this equation gives us a predicted midband gain of 47.5, which is sufficiently close to the measured midband gain for most purposes.

Let us now look back to see that this procedure is very different from what the generic-specific account supposes. We start with a general abstract equation, (3.3); make some approximations; and end with (3.5), which gives rise to detailed phenomenological predictions. Thus superficially it may look like a D-N explanation of the facts predicted. But unlike the covering laws of D-N explanations, (3.3) as it stands is not an equation that really describes the circuits to which it is applied. (3.3) is refined by accounting for the specific causal features of each individual situation to form an equation like (3.5). (3.5) gives rise to accurate predictions, whereas a rigorous solution to (3.3) would be dramatically mistaken.

But one might object: isn't the circuit model, with no resistance added in, just an idealization? And what harm is that? I agree that the circuit model is a very good example of one thing we typically mean by the term idealization. But how can that help the defender of fundamental laws? Most philosophers have made their peace with idealizations: after all, we have been using them in mathematical physics for well over two thousand years. Aristotle in proving that the rainbow is no greater than a semi-circle in Meterologica III. 5 not only treats the sun as a point, but in a blatant falsehood puts the sun and the reflecting medium (and hence the rainbow itself) the same distance from the observer. Today, we still make the same kinds of idealizations in our celestial theories. Nevertheless, we have managed to discover the planet Neptune, and to keep our satellites in space. Idealizations are no threat to the progress of science.

But what solace is this to the realist? How do idealizations save the truth of the fundamental laws? The idea seems to be this. To call a model an idealization is to suggest that the model is a simplification of what occurs in reality, usually a simplification which omits some relevant features, such as the extended mass of the planets or, in the example of the circuit model, the resistance in the bypass capacitor. Sometimes the omitted factors make only an insignificant contribution to the effect under study. But that does not seem to be essential to idealizations, especially to the idealizations that in the end are applied by engineers to study real things. In calling something an idealization it seems not so important that the contributions from omitted factors be small, but that they be ones for which we know how to correct. If the idealization is to be of use, when the time comes to apply it to a real system we had better know how to add back the contributions of the factors that have been left out. In that case the use of idealizations does not seem to counter realism: either the omitted factors do not matter much, or in principle we know how to treat them.

In the sense, the circuit model is patently an idealization. We begin with equation (3.3), which is inadequate; we know the account can be improved—Nordby and how. But the improvements come at the wrong place for the defender of fundamental laws. They come from the ground up, so-to-speak, and not from the top down. We do not modify the treatment by deriving from our theoretical principles a new starting equation to replace (3.3). It is clear that we could not do so, since only part of the fault is diagnosed. What we do instead is to add a phenomenological correction factor, a factor that helps produce a correct description, but that is not dictated by fundamental law.

But could we not 'in principle' make the corrections right at the start, and write down a more accurate equation from the beginning? That is just the assumption of challenge. Even if we could, why do we think that by going further and further backwards, trying to get an equation that will be right when all the significant factors are included, we will eventually get something simple which looks like one of the fundamental laws of our basic theories? Recall the discussion of cross effects in that we usually do not have any uniform procedure for 'adding' interactions. When we try to write down the 'more correct' equations, we get a longer and longer list of complicated laws of different forms, and not the handful of simple equations which could be fundamental in a physical theory.

Generality and simplicity are the substance of explanation. But they are also crucial to application. In engineering, one wants laws with a reasonably wide scope, models that can be used first in one place then another. If right, a law that actually covered any specific case, without much change or correction, would be so specific that it would not be likely to work anywhere else. Recall Bertrand Russell's objection to the 'same cause, same effect' principle:

> The principle 'same cause, same effect,' which philosophers imagine to be vital to science, is therefore utterly otiose. As soon as the antecedents have been given sufficiently fully to enable the consequents to be calculated with some exactitude, the antecedents have become so complicated that it is very unlikely they will ever recur. Hence, if this were the principle involved, science would remain utterly sterile.

Russell's solution is to move to functional laws which state relations between properties (rather than relations between individuals). But the move does not work if we want to treat real, complex situations with precision. Engineers are comfortable with functions. Still they do not seem able to find functional laws that allow them to calculate consequences 'with some exactitude' and yet are not 'so complicated that it is very unlikely they will ever recur'. To find simple laws that we can use again and again, it looks as if we had better settle for laws that patently need improvement. Following Russell, it seems that if we model approximation on D-N explanation, engineering 'would remain utterly sterile'.

1.2. Exponential Decay

The second example concerns the derivation of the exponential decay law in quantum mechanics. But the point wants to stress can be summarized by quoting one of the best standard texts, by Eugen Merzbacher: 'The fact remains that the exponential decay law, for which we have so much empirical support in radioactive processes, is not a rigorous consequence of quantum mechanics but the result of somewhat delicate approximations.'

The exponential decay law is a simple, probabilistically elegant law, for which—as Merzbacher says we have a wealth of experimental support. Yet it cannot be derived exactly in the quantum theory. The exponential law can only be derived by making some significant approximation. In the conventional treatment the rigorous solution is not pure exponential, but includes several additional terms. These additional terms are supposed to be small, and the difference between the rigorous and the approximate solution will be unobservable for any realistic time periods. The fact remains that the data, together with any reasonable criterion of simplicity (and some such criterion must be assumed if we are to generalize from data to laws at all) speak for the truth of an exponential law; but such a law cannot be derived rigorously. Thus it seems that the approximations we make in the derivation take us closer to, not further from, the truth.

There are two standard treatments of exponential decay: the Weisskopf-Wigner treatment, which was developed in their classic paper of 1930, and the more recent Markov treatment, which sees the exponential decay of an excited atom as a special case in the quantum theory of damping. We will look at the more recent treatment first. Here we consider an abstract system weakly coupled to a reservoir. The aim is to derive a general master equation for the evolution of the system. This equation is similar to the evolution equations of classical statistical mechanics. For the specific case in which we are interested, where the system is an excited atom and the reservoir the electromagnetic field, the master equation turns into the Pauli rate equation, which is the analogue of the exponential law when re-excitement may occur:

Pauli equation:

$$\frac{\partial S_i}{\partial t} = -\Gamma_i S_i + \sum_{k \neq i} \omega_{ik} S_k$$

(Here S_j is the occupation probability of the $_j$th state; Γ_j, the inverse of the lifetime; and ω_{jk} is the transition probability from state k to state j.)

The derivation of the master equation is quite involved. we will focus on the critical feature from our point of view—the Markov approximation. Generally, such a derivation begins with the standard second-order perturbation expansion for the state x of the composite, system and reservoir, which in the interaction picture looks like this:

$$\chi(t) = \chi(t_0) + \frac{1}{ih}\int_{t_0}^{t} [V(t' - t_0), \chi(t_0)dt'$$
$$+ \left(\frac{1}{ih}\right)^2 \int_0^{t'} dt''[V(t' - t_0), [V(t'' - t_0), \chi(t_0)]]$$

Notice that the state of the system and reservoir at t depends on its entire past history through the integrals on the right hand side of this equation. The point of the Markov approximation is to derive a differential equation for the state of the system alone such that the change in this state at a time depends only on the facts about the system at *that* time, and not on its past history. This is typically accomplished by two moves: (*i*) extending the time integrals which involve only reservoir correlations to infinity, on the grounds that the correlations in the reservoir are significant for only a short period compared to the periods over which we are observing the system; and (ii) letting $t - t_0 \to 0$, on the grounds that the periods of time considered for the system are small compared to its lifetime. The consequence is a master equation with the desired feature.

We note that the r.h.s. [right hand side] of [the master equation] no longer contains time integrals over S(*t'*) [S is the state of the system alone] for times earlier than the present so that the future is now indeed determined by the present. We have assumed that the reservoir correlation times are zero on a time scale in which the system loses an appreciable amount of its energy. One sometimes refers to the Markoff approximation as a coarse-grained averaging.

Thus the Markov approximation gives rise to the master equation; for an atom in interaction with the electromagnetic field, the master equation specializes to the Pauli equation; and the Pauli equation predicts exponential decay for the atom. Without the Markov approximation, the decay can at best be near exponential.

Let us now look at the Weisskopf-Wigner method, as it is employed nowadays. We begin with the exact Schroedinger equations for the amplitudes, but assume that the only significant coupling is between the excited and the de-excited states:

$$\frac{dc_e}{dt} = \sum_f g_{ef}^2 \int_0^t dt' \exp\{t(\omega_{eg} - \omega_f)(t - t')\} c_e(t')$$

(ω_{eg} is $E_e - E_g/h$, for E_e the energy of the excited state, E_g the energy of the de-excited; ω_f is the frequency of the *f*th mode of the field; and g_{ef} is the coupling constant between the excited state and the *f*th mode. ce is the amplitude in the excited state, no photons present.)

The first approximation notes that the modes of the field available to the de-exciting atom form a near continuum. (We will learn more about this in the next section.) So the sum over *f* can be replaced by an integral, to give

$$\frac{dc_e}{dt} = \int_{-\infty}^{+\infty} -g^2(\omega) D(\omega) d\omega \int_0^t dt' \exp\{i(\omega_{eg} - \omega)(t - t')\} c_e(t').$$

We could now pull out the terms which are slowly varying in ω, and do the ω integral, giving a delta function in *t*:

$$\frac{dc_e}{dt} = g^2(\omega_{eg})D(\omega_{eg})\int_0^t dt' c_e(t') \times \int_{-\infty}^{+\infty} \exp\{i(\omega_{eg} - \omega)(t - t')\} dw$$

$$= g^2(\omega_{eg})D(\omega_{eg})\pi \int_0^t dt' c_e(t')\delta(t - t')$$

or setting $\gamma = 2\Pi g^2(\omega_{eg})D(\omega_{eg})$,

$$\frac{dc_e}{dt} = -\frac{\gamma}{2} c_e(t)$$

and finally,

$$c_e(t) = \exp(-\gamma/2t).$$

But in moving so quickly we lose the Lamb shift—a small displacement in the energy levels discovered by Willis Lamb and R.C. Rutherford in 1947. It will pay to do the integrals in the opposite order. In this case, we note that $c_e(t)$ is itself slowly varying compared to the rapid oscillations from the exponential, and so it can be factored out of the *t'* integral, and the upper limit of that integral can be extended to infinity. Notice that the extension of the *t'* limit is very similar to the Markov approximation already described, and the rationale is similar. We get

$$\frac{dc_e}{dt} = \int_{-\infty}^{+\infty} g^2(\omega)D(\omega)c_e(t)\exp\{i(\omega_{eg} - \omega)t\} dw \times$$

$$\int_{-\infty}^{+\infty} \exp\{-i(\omega_{eg} - \omega)t'\} dt'$$

$$= \int_{-\infty}^{+\infty} g^2(\omega)D(\omega)c_e(t)\exp\{i(\omega_{eg} - \omega)t\} dw$$

$$\left\{\pi\delta(\omega_{eg} - \omega) + iD\left(\frac{1}{\omega_{eg} - \omega}\right)\right\}$$

or, setting $\gamma = 2\Pi g_2(\omega_{eg})D(\omega_{eg})$ and

$$\Delta\omega \equiv -\int_{-\infty}^{+\infty} \frac{g^2(\omega)D(\omega)}{\omega_{eg} - \omega} dw$$

(P (x) = principal part of x.)

$$\frac{dc_e}{dt} = -\left(\frac{\gamma}{2} + i\Delta\omega\right)c_e(t)$$

Here $\Delta\omega$ is the Lamb shift. The second method, which results in a Lamb shift as well as the line-broadening γ, is what is usually now called 'the Weisskopf- Wigner' method.

We can try to be more formal and avoid approximation altogether. The obvious way to proceed is to evaluate the Laplace transform, which turns out to be

$$c_e(s) \equiv \int_0^{\infty} \exp(-st)c_e(t)dt = \frac{1}{s + i\sum_f \left(\frac{g_{ef}^2}{w_{eg} - w_f + is}\right)}$$

then

$$c_e(t) = \frac{1}{2\pi i}\int_{\epsilon - i\infty}^{\epsilon + i\infty} \exp(st)c_e(s)ds$$

To solve this equation, the integrand must be defined on the first and second Riemann sheets. The method is described clearly in Goldberger and Watson's text on collision theory.

The primary contribution will come from a simple pole $\Delta\varepsilon$ such that

$$\frac{i}{\hbar\Delta\in} \equiv \frac{\gamma}{2} + i\Delta\omega = \lim_{s\to 0^+}\sum_f \frac{g_{ef}}{w_{eg} - w_f \_ is}$$

This term will give us the exponential we want:

$$c_e(t) = \exp\left\{-\left(\frac{\gamma}{2} + i\Delta\omega\right)t\right\}$$

But this is not an exact solution. As we distort the contour on the Riemann sheets, we cross other poles which we have not yet considered. We have also neglected the integral around the final contour itself. Goldberger and Watson calculate that this last integral contributes a term proportional to $h^{3/2}/\,t^{3/2}E_e$. They expect that the other poles will add only negligible contributions as well, so that the exact answer will be a close approximation to the exponential law we are seeking; a close approximation, but still only an approximation. If a pure exponential law is to be derived, we had better take our approximations as improvements on the initial Schroedinger equation, and not departures from the truth.

Is there no experimental test that tells which is right? Is decay really exponential, or is the theory correct in predicting departures from the exponential law when t gets large? There was a rash of tests of the experimental decay law in the middle 1970s, spurred by E.T. Jaynes's 'neo-classical' theory of the interaction of matter with the electromagnetic field, a theory that did surprisingly well at treating what before had been thought to be pure quantum phenomena. But these tests were primarily concerned with Jaynes's claim that decay rates would depend on the occupation level of the initial state. The experiments had no bearing on the question of very long time decay behaviour. This is indeed a very difficult question to test. Rolf Winter has experimented on the decay of Mn^{56} up to 34 half-lives, and D.K. Butt and A.R. Wilson on the alpha decay of radon for over 40 half-lives. But, as Winter remarks, these lengths of time, which for ordinary purposes are quite long, are not relevant to the differences I have been discussing, since 'for the radioactive decay of Mn^{56} non-exponential effects should not occur before roughly 200 half-lives. In this example, as with all the usual radioactive decay materials, nothing observable should be left long before the end of the exponential region'. In short, as we read in a 1977 review article by A. Pais, 'experimental situations in which such deviations play a role have not been found to date.' The times before the differences emerge are just too long.

2. Approximations not Dictated by the Facts

Again, it will illustrate with two examples. The examples show how the correct approximation procedure can be undetermined by the facts. Both are cases in which the very same procedure, justified by exactly the same factual claims, gives different results depending on when we apply it: the same approximation applied at different points in the derivation yields two different incompatible predictions. I think this is typical of derivation throughout physics; but in order to avoid spending too much space laying out the details of different cases, it will illustrate with two related phenomena: (*a*) the Lamb shift in the excited state of a single two-level atom; and (*b*) the Lamb shift in the ground state of the atom.

2.1. The Lamb Shift in the Excited State

Consider again spontaneous emission from a two-level atom. The traditional way of treating exponential decay derives from the classic paper of V. Weisskopf and Eugene Wigner in 1930. In its present form the Weisskopf-Wigner method makes three important approximations: (1) the rotating wave approximation; (2) the replacement of a sum by an integral over the modes of the electromagnetic field and the factoring out of terms that vary slowly in the frequency; and (3) factoring out a slowly-varying term from the time integral and extending the limit on the integral to infinity. We will discuss the first approximation below when we come to consider the level shift in the ground state. The second and third are familiar from the last section. Here we want to concentrate on how they affect the Lamb shift in the excited state.

Both approximations are justified by appealing to the physical characteristics of the atom-field pair. The second approximation is reasonable because the modes of the field are supposed to form a near continuum; that is, there is a very large number of very closely spaced modes. This allows us to replace the sum by an integral. The integral is over a product of the coupling constant as a function of the frequency, ω, and a term of the form $\exp(-i\omega t)$. The coupling constant depends on the interaction potential for the atom and the field, and it is supposed to be relatively constant in ω compared to the rapidly oscillating exponential. Hence it can be factored outside the integral with little loss of accuracy. The third approximation is similarly justified by the circumstances.

What is important is that, although each procedure is separately rationalized by appealing to facts about the atom and the field, it makes a difference in what order they are applied. This is just what we saw in the last section. If we begin with the third approximation, and perform the t integral before we use the second approximation to evaluate the sum over the modes, we predict a Lamb shift in the excited state. If we do the approximations and take the integrals in the reverse order—which is essentially what . Weisskopf and Wigner did in their original paper—we lose the Lamb shift. The facts that we cite justify both procedures, but the facts do not tell us in what order to apply them. There is nothing about the physical situation that indicates which order is right other than the fact to be derived: a Lamb shift is observed, so we had best do first (3), then (2). Given all the facts with which we start about the atom and the field and about their interactions, the Lamb shift for the excited state fits the fundamental quantum equations. But we do not derive it from them.

One may object that we are not really using the same approximation in different orders; for, applied at different points, the same technique does not produce the same approximation. True, the coefficients in t and in ω are slowly varying, and factoring them out of the integrals results in only a small error. But the exact size of the error depends on the order in which the integrations are taken. The order that takes first the t integral and then the ω integral is clearly preferable, because it reduces the error.

Two remarks are to be made about this objection. Both have to do with how approximations work in practice. First, in this case it looks practicable to try to calculate and to compare the amounts of error introduced by the two approximations. But often it is practically impossible to decide which of two procedures will lead to more accurate results. For instance, we often justify dropping terms from an equation by showing that the coefficients of the omitted terms are small compared to those of the terms we retain. But as the next example will show, knowing the relative sizes of terms in the equation is not a sure guide to the exact effects in the solution, particularly when the approximation is embedded in a series of other approximations. This is just one simple case. The problem is widespread. Proliferation of treatments is the norm in physics, and very often nobody knows exactly how they compare. When the situation becomes bad enough, whole books may be devoted to sorting it out. Here is just one example, *The Theory of Charge Exchange* by Robert Mapleton. The primary purpose of the book is to explain approximating methods for cross sections and probabilities for electronic capture. But its secondary purpose is to compare different approximate predictions with each other and with experimentally determined values. These comparisons should enable us to determine which approximating procedures are most successful in predicting cross sections for different ranges they also should indicate which methods show most promise for additional improvement.

Comparing approximations is often no easy matter.

Secondly, the objection assumes the principle 'the more accuracy, the better. But this is frequently not so, for a variety of well-known reasons: the initial problem is set only to a given level of accuracy, and any accuracy in the conclusion beyond this level is spurious; or the use of certain mathematical devices, such as complex numbers, will generate excess terms which we do not expect to have any physical significance; and so on. The lesson is this: a finer approximation provides a better account than a rougher one only if the rougher approximation is not good enough. In the case at hand, the finer approximation is now seen to be preferable, not because it produces a quantitatively slightly more accurate treatment, but rather because it exposes a qualitatively significant new phenomenon the Lamb shift in the ground state. If you look back at the equations in the last section it is obvious that the first-ω-then t order misses an imaginary term: the amplitude to remain in the excited state has the form $\exp(-1/2\Gamma t)$ rather than $\exp\{-(1/2\Gamma + i\omega)t\}$. This additional imaginary term, iω, appears when the integrals are done in the reverse order, and it is this term that represents the Lamb shift. But what difference does this term make? In the most immediate application, for calculating decay probabilities, it is completely irrelevant, for the probability is obtained by multiplying together the amplitude $\exp\{-(1/2\Gamma + i\omega)t\}$, and its complex conjugate $\exp\{-(1/2\Gamma - i\omega)t\}$, in which case the imaginary part disappears and we are left with the well-known probability for exponential decay, $\exp(-\Gamma t)$.

The point is borne out historically. The first-ω-then-*t* order, which loses the Lamb shift, is an equivalent approximation to the *ansatz* which Weisskopf and Wigner use in their paper of 1930, and it was the absolutely conventional treatment for seventeen years. To calculate the value of the missing imaginary terms, one has to come face to face with divergences that arise from the Dirac theory of the electron, and which are now so notorious in quantum electrodynamics. These problems were just pushed aside until the remarkable experiments in 1947 by Willis Lamb and his student R. C. Retherford, for which Lamb later won the Nobel prize.

The Dirac theory, taking the spin of the electron into account, predicted an exact coincidence of the $2^2P1/2$ and the $2^2S1/2$ levels. There was a suspicion that this prediction was wrong. New microwave techniques developed during the war showed Lamb a way to find out, using the metastable $2^2S1/2$ state of hydrogen. In the 1947 experiment the Lamb shift was discovered and within a month Bethe had figured a way to deal with the divergences. After the discovery of the Lamb shift the original Weisskopf-Wigner method had to be amended. Now we are careful to take the integrals in the first-t-then-ω order. But look at what Bethe himself has to say:

By very beautiful experiments, Lamb and Retherford have shown that the fine structure of the second quantum state of hydrogen does not agree with the prediction of the Dirac theory. The $2s$ level, which according to Dirac's theory should coincide with the $2p_{1/2}$ level, is actually higher than the latter by an amount of about 0.033 cm^{-1} or 1000 megacycles.

Schwinger and Weisskopf, and Oppenheimer have suggested that a possible explanation might be the shift of energy levels by the interaction of the electron with the radiation field. This shift comes out infinite in all existing theories, and has therefore always been ignored.

Or consider Lamb's comment on Bethe in his Nobel Prize address:

A month later [after 'the fine structure deviations were definitely established experimentally' by Lamb and Retherford], Bethe found that quantum electrodynamics had really hidden behind its divergences a physical content that was in very close agreement with the microwave observations.

Now we attend to the imaginary terms because they have real 'physical content in very close agreement with microwave observations'. But until Lamb's experiments they were just mathematical debris which represented nothing of physical significance and were, correctly, omitted.

2.2. The Lamb Shift in the Ground State

The details of the second example are in G.S. Agarwal's monograph on spontaneous emission. Recall that there are two common methods for treating spontaneous emission. The first is the Weisskopf-Wigner method, and the second is via a Markov approximation, leading to a master equation or a Langevin equation, analogous to those used in classical statistical mechanics. As Agarwal stresses, one reason for preferring the newer statistical approach is that it allows us to derive the Lamb shift in the ground state, which is not predicted by the Weisskopf-Wigner method even after that method has been amended to obtain the shift in the excited state. But we can derive the ground state shift only if we are careful about how we use the rotating wave approximation.

The rotating wave approximation is used when the interaction between radiation and matter is weak. In weak interactions, such as those that give rise to spontaneous emission, the atoms and field can be seen as almost separate systems, so that energy lost by the atoms will be found in the field, and vice versa. Thus virtual transitions in which both the atom and the field simultaneously gain or lose a quantum of energy will have negligible effects. The rotating wave approximation ignores these effects. When the coupling is weak, the terms which represent virtual transitions vary as $\exp\{\pm i(\omega + \omega_k)t\}$ ($h\omega = E_m - E_n$, for energies levels E_m and E_n of the atom; ω_k is a mode frequency of the field). Energy conserving transitions vary as $\exp\{\pm i(\omega - \omega_k)t\}$. For optical frequencies ω_k is large. Thus for ordinary times of observation the $\exp\{\pm i(\omega + \omega_k)t\}$ terms oscillate rapidly, and will average approximately to zero. The approximation is called a 'rotating-wave' approximation because it retains only terms in which the atom and field waves 'rotate together'.

The statistical treatments which give rise to the master equation make an essential use of a Markov approximation. In the last section we see one standard way to derive the Pauli equations, which are the master equations relevant for spontaneous emission. But according to Agarwal, there are two ways to carry through such a derivation, and the results are significantly different depending on where we apply the rotating wave approximation. On the one hand, we can begin with the full Hamiltonian for the interaction of the orbiting electron with the electromagnetic field, and drop from this Hamiltonian the 'counter-rotating' terms which represent virtual transitions, to obtain a shortened approximate Hamiltonian which Agarwal numbers (*2.24*). Then, following through steps like those described above, one obtains a version of the master equation—Agarwal's equation *A. 7*. Alternatively, we can use the full Hamiltonian throughout, dropping the counter-rotating terms only in the last step. This gives us Agarwal's equation (*A. 6*).

What difference do the two methods make to the Lamb shift? Agarwal reports:

> The shift of the ground state is missing from (*A. 7*), mainly due to the virtual transitions which are automatically excluded from the Hamiltonian. The master equation (*A. 6*) obtained by making RWA (the rotating wave approximation) on the master equation rather than on the Hamiltonian does include the shift of the ground state. These remarks make it clear that RWA on the original Hamiltonian is not the same as RWA on the master equation and that one should make RWA on the final equations of motion.

The rotating wave approximation is justified in cases of spontaneous emission by the weakness of the coupling between the atom and the field. But no further features of the interaction determine whether we should apply the approximation to the original Hamiltonian, or whether instead we should apply it to the master equation. Agarwal applies it to the master equation, and he is thus able to derive a Lamb shift in the ground state. But his derivation does not show that the Schroedinger equation dictates a Lamb shift for a two-level atom in weak interaction with an electromagnetic field. The shift is consistent with what the equation says about weak interactions, but it does not follow from it.

This kind of situation is even more strikingly illustrated if we try to calculate the values of the shifts for the twolevel atoms. Lamb and Retherford's experiments, for example, measured the value of the shift for the $2S$ state in hydrogen to be 1057 mega-cycles per second. We can 'derive' a result very close to this in quantum electrodynamics using the technique of mass renornmalization for the electron. But the derivation is notorious: the exact details, in which infinities are subtracted from each other in just the right way to produce a convergent result, are completely *ad hoc*, and yet the quantitative results that they yield are inordinately accurate.

The realist has a defence ready. We say that the Schroedinger equation does not make a claim about whether there is or is not a Lamb shift in the circumstances described. But the realist will reply that we have not described the circumstances as fully as possible. The rotating wave approximations depend on the fact that the interaction between the field and the atom is 'weak'; but if realism is correct, there is a precise answer to the question 'How weak?' The atom-field interaction will have a precise quantitative representation that can in principle be written into the Schroedinger equation. The exact solution to the equation with that term written in will either contain a Lamb shift, or it will not, and that is what the Schroedinger equation says about a Lamb shift in cases of spontaneous emission.

This defence allows us to state more exactly its aims. We do not argue against taking the fundamental laws as true, but try only to counter the most persuasive argument in favour of doing so. As a positive argument in favour of realism, the realist's defence, which plumps for exact solutions and rigorous derivations, gets the logic of the debate out of order. We begin with the challenge, 'Why should we assume that the short abstract equations, which form the core of our fundamental theories, are true at all, even "true enough for now"?' The realist replies 'Because the fundamental equations are so successful at explaining a variety of messy and complicated phenomenological laws'. We say 'Tell me more about explanation. What is there in the explanatory relation which guarantees that the truth of the explanandum argues for the truth of the explanans?' The realist's answer, at least on the plausible generic-specific account, is that the fundamental laws say the same thing as the phenomenological laws which are explained, but the explanatory laws are more abstract and general. Hence the truth of the phenomenological laws is good evidence for the truth of the fundamental laws. I reply to this, 'Why should we think the fundamental and the phenomenological laws say the same thing about the specific situations studied?' and the realist responds, 'Just look at scientific practice. There you will see that phenomenological laws are deducible from the more fundamental laws that explain them, once a description of the circumstances is given.'

We have just been looking in detail at cases of scientific practice, cases which I think are fairly typical. Realists can indeed put a gloss on these examples that brings them into line with realist assumptions: rigorous solutions to exact equations might possibly reproduce the correct phenomenological laws with no ambiguity 'when the right equations are found'. But the reason for believing in this gloss is not the practice itself, which we have been looking at, but rather the realist metaphysics, which we began by challenging. Examples of the sort we have considered here could at best be thought consistent with realist assumptions, but they do not argue for them.

Summary

Fundamental laws are supposed by many to determine what phenomenological laws are true. If the primary argument for this view is the practical explanatory success of the fundamental laws, the conclusion should be just the reverse. We have a very large number of phenomenological laws in all areas of applied physics and engineering that give highly accurate, detailed descriptions of what happens in realistic situations. In an explanatory treatment these are derived from fundamental laws only by a long series of approximations and emendations. Almost always the emendations improve on the dictates of the fundamental law; and even where the fundamental laws are kept in their original form, the steps of the derivation are frequently not dictated by the facts. This makes serious trouble for the D-N model, the generic-specific account, and the view that fundamental laws are better. When it comes to describing the real world, phenomenological laws win out.

❑❑❑

4

Foundations Problems in General Relativity

Introduction

Isaac Newton made the theory of gravitation the paradigm of all physical theories. Using relatively modest information summarized in Kepler's laws of planetary motion, and realizing that the same force that governed the trajectories of the celestial bodies also is responsible for the free fall of apples on earth, he evolved a quantitative theory of the gravitational interaction of all objects possessing mass. This theory explained all known facts of gravitationally controlled motion (with the exception of Mercury's perihelion advance) through three centuries and, moreover, made it possible to predict details of planetary and satellite trajectories centuries ahead. Even in designing the trajectories of today's space vehicles, determining their launching parameters, and calculating required orbit corrections, space technologists have found Newton's equations work perfectly.

Today's prevailing theory of gravitation, the general theory of relativity, did not grow out of any failure of Newton's equations (though it explains the one slight discrepancy on Mercury's orbit, which had been discovered in mid-nineteenth century), but resulted from an attempt to reconcile the two contradictory sets of notions of space and time appropriate to Newton's theories and to an account of electromagnetic phenomena, respectively.

Briefly, Newton considered time as universal, and as being held in common by all reasonable frames of reference. He took it for granted that the notion of simultaneity of two (distant) events was unrelated to the state of motion of the observer, or of the instrumentation used to determine, for instance, which (if any) of two events preceded the other in time.

In electrodynamics, signals, or any other disturbances of an established condition of the field, spread at a finite speed, the speed of light. Information about two distant events can be correlated only if this information is physically propagated to a common site, where comparisons can then be made by man or instrument. For events that are not too widely separated from each other in time (specifically, they must be so nearly simultaneous that a flash announcing the occurrence of either will not reach the site of the other before that second event takes place), the motion of the instrument used for comparison determines which of these two events is considered to have taken place first. As a result, synchronization of clocks that are in relative motion, or merely distant from each other, depends on how the synchronization is performed, in a manner that can be predicted on the strength of the hypothesis that to any observer in whatever state of (uniform, rectilinear) motion the speed of light has the universal value $c = 3 \times 1010$ cm sec^{-1}.

That the speed of light is indeed a universal constant is confirmed by a wealth of observational evidence. The resulting dependence of time and distance determinations on the state of motion of the observer is systematized in the so-called special theory of relativity. The corner stone of Newtonian mechanics is the instantaneous reach of forces from one massive body to another ("action at a distance"), and this reach requires absolute simultaneity. Thus two conflicting space-time structures (or models) arose from theories, each of which was phenomenally successful in its area of applicability.

It was to reconcile this conflict that Einstein formulated the general theory of relativity. In the first instance this new theory deals with gravitation; it modifies Newton's mechanical approach and replaces action at a distance with a new field, which mediates the interactions between massive bodies. Disturbances of a gravitational nature in this field theory will propagate at a finite rate, the same rate at which electromagnetic phenomena spread. The velocities of heavenly bodies in our solar system are sufficiently small so that the deviations from Newton's laws resulting from the field interpretation are too minute in almost all instances to be observable with classical techniques. If this were all the innovation brought about by general relativity, it would have set to rest any worries about a self-contradictory space-time picture, but would not have been memorable as a new departure.

The novel idea of general relativity has been the incorporation of an ancient discovery into the foundations of gravitational theory; this is the fact that in a field of gravity all bodies undergo the same acceleration. As a result, it is not possible to separate by local experiment the influence of gravity from the possible intrinsic accelerations of a frame of reference; inertial frames of reference can be established only by reference to global considerations, i.e. in practice by the use of astronomical information. By hypothesizing that even global techniques might break down, Einstein destroyed the hitherto preeminent role of the inertial frames of reference and of the transformations connecting inertial frames.

Thus, in the first instance, the topological manifold that we know as space-time is deprived of its previous rigidity (the Minkowski universe) and endowed, instead, with the possibility of a rich geometric structure, which might be the carrier of physical properties. In this sense general relativity has fused geometry and physics. The actual structure adopted by Einstein, principally on the grounds of a correspondence with the earlier Minkowski geometry, was an indefinite, pseudo-Riemannian metric, which carries with it not only a quadratic norm for infinitesimal displacement vector fields, but also an affine connection and a curvature. The dynamical laws proposed by Einstein consist of a connection between the local curvature and the sources of the gravitational field, that is to say masses, mass flux, and stress. As a physical theory general relativity has been completely successful: Wherever its predictions deviate from those of Newtonian physics, experiments have confirmed the presence of these "relativistic effects".

Einstein's genius enabled him to formulate the most conservative hypothesis on space-time geometry compatible with the non-existence of a rigid (pseudo-Euclidean) geometry that accounted for the known facts. There is no reason to believe, and neither did Einstein himself believe, that his theory will endure without modifications as experimental techniques are increasingly refined. Even from a conceptual point of view, once the traditional space-time notions have been subjected to questioning, further generalizations almost offer themselves to our speculations.

Unified field theories have been proposed, by Einstein and by others, in which the space-time manifold is endowed with a variety of geometric structures, so that one might combine the dynamics of the gravitational field with all other known physical fields, i.e. with the electromagnetic and, today, with the lepton and hadron fields. Some unified field theories go beyond the four-dimensionality of space-time and conjecture additional dimensions, which are then restricted by the assumption of isometries or near-isometries, so as to account for the observed four dimensionality.

Even within general relativity there is the possibility of true singularities of space-time, i.e. regions in which the regular metric structure breaks down. Such a break-down implies that at the very least the partial differential equations that form the field laws of general relativity are not satisfied in the singular regions. Either all "local" solutions of the field laws whose continuation in space-time leads to singularities must be excluded as "unphysical", or else the true laws of nature are less restrictive than the field equations; they are equivalent to the field equations only under circumstances that do not obtain everywhere. That the highly non-linear partial differential equations of general relativity frequently, and inevitably, involve the appearance of singularities gives rise to questions as to the ultimate validity of the field equations, and their appropriateness as the mathematical formulation of the laws of nature.

Another aspect of the equations of general relativity is that at least some solutions of the field equations imply space-time topologies that deviate grossly from what is ordinarily called Euclidean manifolds. Not only the metric properties of space-time are made subject to dynamical laws but the very connectedness of that continuum. These complexities have been referred to, variously, as Einstein-Rosen bridges, as wormholes, and as Swiss cheese models, depending on the character of the space-time contortions assumed.

One might go a step further. General relativity dispenses with rectilinear coordinate systems but retains the notion that the space-time continuum is composed of points, which in their turn form (topological) neighborhoods, or open sets. The continuous and differentiable mappings of the space-time manifold on itself imply and justify the continuing role of continuous and differentiable coordinate transformations. The laws of nature, according to general relativity, are to be invariant under this class of transformations, because intrinsically all points, and all neighborhoods of the space-time continuum are equivalent. But whereas the appearance of singularities and of exotic topologies challenges the supposed equivalence of all world points, their very existence as intrinsic objects is called into doubt by the existence of coordinate transformations that do not map point onto point, but rather field onto field.

To explain this point properly, it is necessary to make a distinction between several different types of (curvilinear) coordinate transformations. Presumably a coordinate transformation may be regarded as an instruction to map every point of a manifold uniquely, and reversibly, on another point. As long as the instruction makes no reference to the field at that point (or elsewhere), this is a normal point-to-point mapping, and these mappings form a group (or a groupoid). But it is also possible to conceive of an instruction that relates the point-to-point mapping to the field (metric or otherwise) defined on the manifold. As a result of that mapping, the field changes as well, according to its own transformation law (e.g. that of a tensor field); this change must be taken into consideration if two such mappings are to be performed in succession. To study the structure of the resulting group (or groupoid) one is better off thinking of the mapping of the function space of possible fields on itself, in other words the instruction maps field onto field. This more sophisticated kind of coordinate transformation contains the straight point-to-point mapping as a subgroup. The remarkable fact is that general relativistic theories are invariant with respect to coordinate transformations both of the straight point-to-point variety and of the more general kind.

The situation may be likened to the well-known difference, in classical mechanics, between the Lagrangian and the Hamiltonian formalism. Canonical transformations map a point in configuration space on another in configuration space, but uniquely only if we also know the values of the momentum components. That is to say, points possessing the same q-coordinates but different p-coordinates are mapped on points having different q-coordinates as well. Hence, under canonical transformations the points of configuration space lose their intrinsic identities, they do not form invariant subspaces in phase space. This is precisely the case with world points under the more general coordinate transformations: A world point (identified by its coordinate values or, perhaps, by its geometric properties) gets mapped on a definite world point only if the field is fixed; clothed with different fields it will get mapped on different world points. In this sense one may speak quite appropriately of the evanescent nature of the world point under the more general type of coordinate transformation.

One should not exaggerate the degree of disappearance of the identifiable world point. The function space mappings with respect to which the theory is invariant are still those that may be described as coordinate transformations, or as point mappings. One may, however, contemplate the possibility of theories beyond the framework of current field theories, theories that will have wider, or simply different invariance groups. What is needed is a physical and intuitive clue pointing the way.

Another investigation is aimed at accomodating general relativity to other physical theories, which nowadays are quantum field theories. Though presently gravitational radiation can be observed only marginally, in the not too distant future it will undoubtedly be possible to observe individual quanta of gravitational radiation. Theoretically, one should be able to predict both the kind of variables that cannot be observed in pairs with arbitrarily high accuracy, and those variables that have discrete spectra. But the elaboration of a quantum theory of gravitation is beset with special difficulties. Some of these are undoubtedly technical, in view of the high degree of non-linearity of Einstein's field dispose of a rigid space-time scaffolding, which, for instance, permits the setting-up of definite Lorentz-invariant propagators. In general relativity this background scaffolding does not exist.

If one accepts the spirit of the theory, there can be no such thing as a classical background metric, though there will be (non-local) constants of the motion. It would seem sensible to reformulate the theory in such a manner that all statements and predictions are independent of the choice of coordinate system. Such an endeavor leads one, almost by compelling force, to the adoption of the field over the four-dimensional manifold, rather than of the manifold by itself, as the physically meaningful object to be considered. At least some of the approaches adopted are in accord with the argument presented previously, to the effect that world points are pale and elusive objects.

In spite of sustained efforts, a definitive and generally accepted quantum theory of gravitation does not as yet exist. Opinions vary as to what features such a theory should possess in order to be universally acceptable. Some serious workers consider the whole program of quantization unsound; they would prefer to retain a classical metric field, which would serve as a backdrop to all non-gravitational physical force fields. The non-gravitational fields are, however, to be quantized. If the gravitational field is to be quantized along with all other fields, opinions differ as to whether such a theory should possess an invariance group of the scope of the group of curvilinear transformations, or whether it should be merely Poincare-invariant. Finally, it is not at all clear whether the topological aspects of space-time are to be quantized, or whether a quantum state should resemble an ensemble of (classical) metric fields all defined on homeomorphic point sets. Most of the workers in this field, including the present author, have strong but differing opinions on all of these points; the very fact that there is disagreement would seem to indicate that so far these opinions should be regarded as just that, not as universally agreed-to principles.

In the absence of a complete quantum theory of gravitation, one may attempt to obtain some tentative ideas on the scope of indeterminacy relations in the final theory. Guidance is provided by the Poisson brackets of the classical theory. Poisson brackets can be defined between constants of the motion, and presumably approximate brackets between approximate constants of the motion. Admittedly, approximate results are no more to be trusted than the underlying approximation or perturbation approaches. Relatively little actual calculations have been done. One calculation, which was not approximate but based on the notion of observables by intrinsic coordinates (also known as coincidences), has resulted in Poisson brackets between components of the metric tensor so involved that intuitive interpretations were not practicable.

Another interesting question involves the recognition of observables with discrete spectra. Recently we have proposed, for a preliminary survey, a phase integral quantization scheme of the kind that held sway before 1925. To formulate such phase integrals one need not appeal to perturbative ("weak-field") notions but merely to topological properties of certain sub-manifolds of the phase space. This program has not yet progressed far enough that I dare predict its ultimate utility. To summarize, theoretical research in gravitation theory, aside from its astronomical and cosmological implications, which I have not even mentioned in this article, challenges our traditional views of space and time, of point sets, and of geometry underlying our theory-making in the physical sciences, and suggests new departures to those who have a bent for speculating along these lines.

❑❑❑

5

Dimensions and Units of Physical Quantities

Introduction

Every physicist knows how to perform a dimensional analysis and how to calculate the units of a dimensionally complex magnitude, but no theory proper has hitherto justified these operations. Worse: the two concepts are often mixed up. Even worse: they are frequently "defined" by reference to measurement operations. In this paper an algebra of dimensions and an algebra of units are built with elementary set theoretic and algebraic resources. By supplying unambiguous and exact elucidations of the concepts of dimension and of unit, those theories may contribute to clearing up some of the confusions that becloud the subject.

1. Dimensions

1.1 Introduction

Dimensional analysis is an established branch of the foundations of physics. However, it is more of a loose collection of concepts, theorems and rules than a hypothetico-deductive system. It is much in the same state as Heavisides's "operational calculus" before it was legitimated by the theory of Laplace transforms. So much so that dimensional analysis does not even supply a mathematical analysis of the very notion of a dimension. Consequently we operate "symbolically", i.e. *de facto* but not *de jure*, with dimensions without quite knowing what they are. We thereby espouse, tacitly to be sure, the pragmatist motto "Things are what they do". This attitude, suitable as it may be for gadgets, is dangerous with regard to ideas.

In this section we provide a justification for the calculus of dimensions. The basic idea, first adumbrated in, is this. Consider the set Q of all physical quantities: durations, entropies, state functions, dimensional constants, and so on and so forth. These concepts sort themselves out into dimension species such as the class L of all length-like quantities: heights, depths, widths, wavelengths, mean free paths, etc. In other words, there is a certain equivalence relation $\equiv$ that induces a partition of the totality Q of physical quantities into homogeneous subsets (species) so that, if q and q' are in Q, then: $q = q'$ if and only if q and q' are of the same species, say L(for length-like), or T(for time-like), or 1_D (for dimensionless). The relation = of equi dimensionality is determined by a certain function on Q that assigns every physical quantity its proper dimensional niche. This function, usually designated by [ ], will be called the dimension function. The value of this function at a physical quantity is precisely some dimension species. For example, the dimension value of a wavelength λ is the dimension species L, i.e. $[\lambda] = L$. What follows is a systematic elaboration of this idea.

1.2 Physical Quantity

Every physical theory is a set of formulas built with certain basic functions and constants called physical quantities. At least one of these must be a magnitude, i.e. a function concerning, or referring to, one or more physical systems and taking values in a subset of real numbers or in a family of intervals of real numbers. (A complex valued function referring to some physical entity will count as two magnitudes and every component of a tensor may be regarded as one magnitude provided it concerns some physical system or other.) In other words, any function $P: A \times B \times ? \times N \rightarrow V$, where V is included in the real line R or in its power set IP(R), is a *magnitude* provided at least one of the cartesian factors A through N is a kind of physical system, e.g. the set of all magnetic fields, or the set of all Carbon molecules. This characterization of a magnitude will suffice here. A more precise definition will be introduced in Section 2.2 in relation with the concept of a unit.

Call

$$Q_T^*$$

the set of basic (undefined) physical quantities in a theory T, with the understanding that

$$Q_T^*$$

includes a nonempty set of magnitudes, or quantities with a factual (e.g. physical) referent. With the help of mathematics any number of derived (defined) physical quantities can be built out of

$$Q_T^*.$$

Call Q_T the infinite set of physical quantities, basic or derived, in a theory T. (Q_T has at least the group structure, but this will not concern us here.) And call Q an arbitrary set of physical quantities: either a subset of a certain Q_T or the union of any number of Q_T's.

In addition to its peculiar set

$$Q_T^*$$

of basic physical quantities, every physical theory T contains a set

D_T^*

of basic dimension values such as *L*, *T*, and *M*. (There is no direct relation between

Q_T^*

and

D_T^*: the asterisk indicates only that the elements of these basic sets are not definable within *T*.) Loosely speaking

D_T^*

is the generator of the totality D_T of dimension values of *T*. This enlarged set D_T includes all the rational powers of the elements of

D_T^*

as well as their finite concatenations, e.g. $L^{3/4}T^{8/5}M^{-2/9}$. Our first task will be to tame D_T. Later on we shall investigate the manner in which each Q_T is associated to its D_T.

1.3 Dimension Value

We start by laying down through Axiom 1:

Axiom 1. For every set *Q* of physical quantities there is a finite set

$$D_Q^* = \{A, B, \ldots, N\}$$

of independent elements called the *basic dimensions values* associated with *Q*.

Next we postulate that the basic dimension values can be raised to rational powers as if they were real numbers. That is, if

$$X \in D_Q^*$$

and if *m* and *n* are natural numbers, then

$X^0 = 1_D X^{-1} \cdot X = X \cdot X^{-1} = 1_D X^{n+1} = X^n \times XX^{-n} = (X^n)^{-1}\ X^{m+n} = X^m \times X^n X^{-m-n} = X^{-m} \times X^{-n}\ (X^m)^n = X^{mn}\ (X^m)^{-n} = X^{-mn}\ Y = X^{1/n} =df\ Y^n = XX^{-1/n} = (X^{-1})^{1/n}\ X^{m/n} = (X^m)^{1/n} X^{-m/n} = (X^{-m})^{1/n}$.

We compress the preceding formulas into following axiom

Axiom 2. Let X be a basic dimension value. Then the structure

$D_X = <D_X, \cdot, ^{-1}, 1_D>$,

where $D_X = \{X\alpha \mid \alpha \text{ rational}\}$, $\cdot$ a binary operation on D_X, $^{-1}$ a unary operation on D_X, and 1_D a distinguished element of D_X, is an abelian group, written multiplicatively, in which the powers are defined just as in the field of reals.

The basic set of this group, i.e. D_X, is constituted by all of the rational powers of the dimension value *X*. It deserves a special name as assigned by

Definition 1. Let $X \in D_Q^*$

Then the set $D_X = \{X^\lambda 1 \text{ rational}\}$ is called the dimension genus *X*.

1.4. System of Dimension Values

We now extend D_X to the set of all dimension values, basic and derived, formed from a given set

D_Q^*

of basic dimension values. That is, we proceed to sanction operations such as $X\alpha \cdot Y\beta$, where *X* and *Y* are dimension values, and α, β rationals. We do this by means of

Axiom 3. Let *Q* be a set of physical quantities and let

D_Q^*

be the associated set of basic dimension values. Then the structure $D_Q = <D_Q, \cdot, ^{-1}\ 1_D>$, where $D_Q = \{A\alpha \cdot B\beta \ldots \cdot N^V /$ *A*, *B*, . . .,

$N \in D_Q^*$

and $\alpha, \beta, \ldots, \upsilon 1^*$ rationals), $\cdot$ a binary operation on D_Q, -1 a unary operation on D_Q, and 1_D a selected element of D_Q, is an abelian group written multiplicatively.

In other words, the infinite set D_Q of all dimension values associated with any given set Q of physical quantities is assumed to have the group structure. We call it the *system of dimension values of Q*.

Let us now find out the relations between the dimension genera D_X (Definition 1) and the totality D_Q of dimension values. Clearly, every one of the former is included in the latter. More precisely, we have

Theorem 1. Let Q be a set of physical quantities and let D_Q be its set of dimension values. Then, for every $X \in D_Q$, $D_X \subseteq D_Q$.

Furthermore every D_Q can be split into as many factors as basic dimension values. More exactly, we shall prove

Theorem 2. Let Q be a set of physical quantities, D_Q its associated set of dimension values, and $D_X = \langle D_X, \cdot, -1, 1_D \rangle$ the group of dimension values of genus $X \in D_Q$. Then the system D_Q of dimension values of Q is the direct product of the dimension genera: $D_Q = D_A \times D_B \times \ldots \times D_N$.

Proof. By Axiom 2 every factor is an abelian group and by Theorem 1 it is included in D_Q. By Axiom 3 the products are commutative. Finally the only element all n factors share is 1_D. So the conditions for a direct product of groups are met.

So far, a dimension value is just an element of a certain group associated with a set of physical quantities. The nature of the elements of this group will become clearer as we find out the kind of association they hold with Q, a task we now turn to.

1.5 Dimension Function

We introduce the dimension function, relating Q to D_Q, through following axiom 4:

Axiom 4. Let Q be a set of physical quantities and D_Q the system of dimension values of Q. The dimension function $[\,]: Q \rightarrow D_Q$ assigns each physical quantity $q \in Q$ a dimension value $d \in D_Q$ in such a way that

(*i*) $[1] = 1_D$.

(*ii*) if $p, q \in Q$, and α, β are rationals, then

$[p\alpha \cdot q^2] = [p\pm] \cdot [q^2]$.

This postulate entails all the desired formal properties of the dimension function. Among them those stated in the following:

Corollary. If p and q are physical quantities, then

(*i*) $[p \cdot q] = [p] \cdot [q]$

(*ii*) $[p \cdot q_{-1}] = [p] \cdot [q]_{-1}$.

The pre systematic notion of dimension has now been split into the clear cut concepts of dimension function and dimension value. And these will in turn help us define a few other standard concepts such as those of dimensionless quantity and dimensional constant:

Definition 2. Any $q \in Q$ for which $[q] = 1_D$ is called a dimensionless quantity.

Definition 3. A scalar with a dimension value other than 1_D is called a *dimensional constant or scale factor.*

A possible partition of a set of physical quantities is into dimensional and dimensionless. A second partition is into dimensional constants (a subset of dimensional quantities) and magnitudes. While dimensional constants concern no physical system (they have no physical referents), magnitudes are associated with definite kinds of physical system. Thus the gravitational constant is a dimensional constant not a property of a physical system, and this both in the classical theory of gravitation and in Einstein's general relativity. A third possible partition of a set of physical quantities is into dimension genera. Indeed, the Definition 1 of dimension genus D_X and Axiom 4 allow us to introduce an equivalence relation ~, interpretable as equivalence in respect of dimensional genus, namely thus:

Definition 4. If p, q ~ Q, then:p ~ q iff $[p]$, $[q] \in D_X$.

For example, $L^{1/2} \sim L^{-3/7}$. But we are more interested in a different, far more natural partition of Q, which shall be introduced presently.

1.6 Equidimensionality and Physical Quantity Species

Consider the set Q of all physical quantities, basic and derived, occurring in all possible physical theories. In order to class them according to their dimension value, i.e. to partition Q into dimension species, we need the equidimensionality relation. This relation, which shall be designated by ≡, is generated by the dimension function [ ], introduced by Axiom 4, according to the following:

Definition 5. If p, q ? Q, then p and q are said to be *equidimensional* iff they have the same dimension value, i.e.

$p = q$ iff $[p] = [q]$.

We can easily prove the following trivial.

Theorem 3. The equidimensionality relation ≡ is an equivalence relation [i.e. it is reflexive, symmetrical and transitive] on Q.

In other words, ≡ is the equivalence kernel of [ ] and as such it is the relation competent to group physical quantities into dimensionally homogeneous species. Every such class is an equivalence class: we shall call it a dimension species. More explicitly, we stipulate:

Definition 6. If $q \in Q$, then the equivalence class of all the ≡ relatives [or species partners] of q is the *dimension species* of q.

By a happy coincidence the standard notation for the equivalence class generated by an element [$q \in Q$ is $[q]$, the same as for the dimension value of q. We shall prove the identity of these two concepts. But to this end we must take a deeper look at the dimensional partition of Q.

1.7 Dimension Value and Dimension Species

Consider the natural dimensional partition of Q, i.e. the partition of Q induced by the equi-dimensionality relation $\equiv$. This is the quotient set of Q by $\equiv$, i.e. $Q/\equiv$, the *family of all physical quantity species*. There is a function that assigns each q in Q the equivalence class $[q]$ in $Q/\equiv$. This function is none other than the dimension function. In other words, we have:

Theorem 4. The dimension function is the projection of Q onto the dimensional partition of Q, i.e.

$[\,]: Q \rightarrow Q/\equiv$, with $[q] = \{p \mid p \in Q \text{ and } p \equiv q\}$

or, equivalently, $[q] = p \equiv q$, where $p \equiv$ denotes the projection map.

Theorem 5. The set of dimension values is equal to the family of all dimension species: $D = Q/\equiv$.

Finally, by the principle of extensionality of set theory, we obtain:

Theorem 6. If $q \in Q$, then the dimension value of q is the same as the dimension species of q.

The last theorem justifies using the same symbol, namely $[q]$, to designate both the dimension value and the dimension species of a physical quantity q.

This winds up our axiomatic theory of the dimensions of physical quantities. Let us see whether it is of any use in assigning dimension values — a practical goal of dimensional analysis.

1.8 The Assignment of Dimension Values

Our theory does not replace the usual dimensional analysis but intends to give it a foundation. The function of our theory is indeed only to elucidate the general notions of dimension in precise mathematical terms. It performs this task without committing itself as to the memberships of the sets Q and D. Consequently our theory is insufficient to determine the dimension value of every physical quantity. Axiom 4 and its logical consequences will determine the dimension of a compound physical quantity, such as the Coulomb force, provided the dimensions of its ingredients (electric charge, dielectric constant, and mutual distance) be given. Now, assigning specific dimension values to simple or unanalyzed physical quantities is a task for specific postulates. In most cases this is felt to be unnecessary because we can recognize intuitively the dimension of a basic familiar quantity. But in some cases (e. g. the dielectric constant) there are ambiguities: different dimension values can be postulated and correspondingly slightly different theories will be possible. In such cases an explicit dimension assignment will be mandatory. Once such an assignment has been made for the unanalyzed quantities, Axiom 4 will yield the dimension of any multiplicatively composed quantity. We may thus jump to the following general prescriptions.

Rule 1. In an axiomatic reconstruction of a physical theory, all those and only those basic (undefined) physical quantities that are not analyzed in that theory should be assigned a dimension value by postulate.

Rule 2. In an informal presentation of a physical theory, only the dimensional constants (e.g. the Boltzmann constant) and those magnitudes for which dimensional ambiguities may arise need be assigned dimension values by explicit hypothesis.

1.9 Conclusion

We have proposed a mathematical theory of the dimensions of physical quantities based on the concepts of physical quantity, dimension value, and dimension function. The formal properties of the last two concepts have been postulated so as to retrieve the usual rules of thumb of the calculus of dimensions. Every dimension value is a set and more precisely an equivalence class. And every system of dimension values is a commutative group. The dimension function defines an equivalence relation = interpretable as the relation of equi-dimensionality. This relation allows us to improve on the initial characterization of a dimension value: it is also a species belonging to the natural dimensional partition $Q/\equiv$.

The veil of mystery that shrouds the intuitive concept of a dimension has thus been lifted, revealing a modest but neat mathematical structure. The question "What are dimensions?" is seen to be ill conceived, for there are two concepts of dimension, namely those of dimension function and dimension value. The correct question is: "What are [ ] and *d*?" The answer is just this: "They are the mathematical objects satisfying the theory expounded above." Admittedly this answer fails to give us a "feel" for dimensions. But the same holds for every other basic concept: While theory alone supplies exactness, only practice breeds familiarity.

2. Units

2.1 Introduction

The concept of a unit is one of those scientific notions that has remained obscure for want of a theory and excess of a coarse philosophy. Indeed we know how to manipulate units but we do not seem to know what kind of mathematical object they are. As a consequence units are sometimes confused with dimensions, at other times with standards, and they are often introduced in relation to measurement rather than to concept formation. Being a theoretical concept, the notion of a unit should be elucidated within a theory proper. And being a generic notion, i.e. one occurring in every branch of quantitative science, its elucidation through a mathematical theory is a task for the foundations of science. What holds for units holds for any expression containing them, such as '3 sec' and '1 barn = 10^{-24} cm^2. Such "symbolic" expressions make no sense at all unless they are embedded in definite algebraic structures sanctioning the usual operations among units and among units and numbers. Let us investigate these structures.

2.2 Units and Coherent Systems of Units

Our starting point must be the concept of a magnitude, for the values of a magnitude are reckoned on some system of units and, conversely, a unit exists only by virtue of its association with a set of magnitudes. (Example: No length value without a length unit and no length unit without a length concept.)

Axiom 5. Let *A*, *B*, . . ., *N* be *n* kinds of physical system, where n is a positive integer. And let *R* designate the real line and IP(*R*) the power set of *R*. Then there exists a nonempty set U_P, called the set of *P-units*, and there is at least one function

$P: A \times B \times ? \times N \times U_P \rightarrow V$, where $V \subseteq R$ or $V \subseteq IP(R)$, called a *magnitude*, such that *P* represents a (mutual) property of every *n*-tuple <*a*, *b*, . . ., *n*> with $a \in A$, $b \in B$, . . ., $n \in N$.

In plain words: every physical system, whether simple or complex, is characterized by properties represent able as real functions, and the values of these functions depend not only on the system itself but also on the units that have been adopted conventionally. For example, in non relativistic mechanics mass is represented by a certain function $M: B \times U_M \rightarrow R+$, where *B* is the set of bodies and U_M the set of mass units. The precise properties of that function *M* are given by the postulates in which *M* occurs. Let us now get a step closer to the conventional ingredient in a magnitude. We first stipulate.

Definition 7. Let *M* be a set of magnitudes. Then the set U_M of units for *M* is the union of the sets of *X*-units for $X \in M$, i.e.

$$U_M = \bigcup_{X \in M} U_X$$

Now, units can be basic (simple) or derived (compound). Thus cm is simple and cm^2 sec^{-1} is compound. And given any set of units there are many ways of analyzing them into simpler units. In short, there are many systems of basic units, such as (cm, g, sec) and {ft, 1b, day}. We consecrate this fact of life, or rather convention, by postulating.

Axiom 6. Let *M* be a set of magnitudes and U_M the set of units for *M*. Then there is at least one nonempty finite subset

$$U_M^* = \{u_1^*, u_2^*, \ldots, u_m^*, 1_U\} \subset U_M$$

called a system of basic units for *M*, such that

(*i*) the elements of U_M are mutually independent (not interdefinable);

(*ii*) the structure

$$U_M^* = \left\langle U_M^*, \bullet, ^{-1}, 1_U \right\rangle$$

is an abelian group written multiplicatively, in which the powers are defined as in the field of reals;

(*iii*) for every $u \in U_M$ there is a μ-tuple < α, β, . . ., > of rational numbers such that u is uniquely decomposable in the form.

$$u = u_1^{*\alpha} \bullet u_2^{*\beta} \bullet \ldots \bullet u_m^{*\mu}$$

Finally we individualize, within the population U_M, the units of a feather, i.e. the coherent systems of units. This task is performed by.

Definition 8. Let *M* be a set of magnitudes and U_M the set of all of its units. Then the structure

$$U_M^C = \left\langle U_M^C, \bullet, ^{-1}, 1_U \right\rangle,$$

with

$$U_M^C \subseteq U_M,$$

is called a *coherent system of units* for *M* if and only if it is an abelian group (written multiplicatively).

In other words, the members of a coherent system of units have inverses and they concatenate freely even if they are not basic units. The belonging to the same coherent system of units, as is the case with $cm^{1/2}$ and $sec^{-3/7}$, defines an equivalence relation E on U_M. In turn this equivalence relation induces the partition U_M / E of any set of units into coherent systems. But we shall not pursue this line here. If we wish to compound units we must choose them from a coherent system. But the injunction to employ only coherent systems of units in any given theory is the subject of a methodological rule that falls outside the algebra of units. Whether or not the rule is implemented, units are uniquely characterized by the above axioms and definitions, which moreover legitimate the "symbolic" operations with units within a coherent system. Our next task will be to legitimate the equally "symbolic" multiplications of numbers by units.

2.3 Denominate Numbers

We shall presently justify the common practice of writing expressions of the form "$r\,u$", where r is some real number (the *numeric* of the magnitude concerned) and u an element of some set U_M of units for the given magnitude. The usual justification is success. Ours will consist in introducing an algebraic structure making room for the totality of expressions of the form "$r\,u$". This structure, to be called an R-group, may be thought of as a merger of a coherent system of units with the field of reals. It must be something more complex than the direct product of the real line (regarded as a group) and a group of units, these two structures do not share the same unit element: $1 \neq 1_U$. We start by defining an R-group. It constitutes the multiplicative partner of an R-module, itself an additive abelian group equipped with scalar multiplication or, rather, multiplication by the elements of a ring of scalars. More precisely, we stipulate.

Definition 9. The structure $R = \langle R, S, f, \cdot, 0, {}^{-1}, 1_S \rangle$ is an *R-group* if and only if (*i*) $< R, +, \cdot, 1 >$ is a commutative ring with unit element 1;

(*ii*) $< S, 0, ^{-1}, 1_S >$ is a multiplicative abelian group with unit element 1_S;

(*iii*) f is a function from $R \times S$ into S, written $<r, s> \to rs = s' \in S$, subject to the following conditions:

(*a*) for every $r \in R$ and any $s, s' \in S$: $r(ss') = (r\,s)\,s' = s(r\,s')$;

(*b*) for any $r, r'\, R$ and every $s \in S$: $(r\,r')\,s = r(r'\,s)$;

(*c*) for every $r \in R$: $r\,1_S = r$.

Note that, since S is a multiplicative group, the addition of arbitrary elements of it is not defined. Nor do we wish to sanction expressions like "$r\,s + r'\,s'$", which could be interpreted as sums of heterogeneous denominate numbers. Sums of denominate numbers make sense only if a unit can be factored out of them, as with "2 cm + 3 cm". To account for this case we define a new operation +' in the set S by means of:

Definition 10. For any $r, r' \in R$ and any $s \in S$, $r\,s +' r'\,s = (r + r')\,s$.

Finally, we restrict the function f occurring in Definition 9 to $R \times T$, where T is a subset of S, and call g the new function. Explicitly: we introduce

Definition 11. Let $T \subset S$, where S is the second set occurring in an R-group, and let f be the function involved in the latter. Then $g = f | R \times T$.

We are now ready to apply these concepts to our problem. We make the following assignments:

R: = The real line.

S: = The totality of denominate numbers of the form "$r\,u$" with $r \in R$ and

$u \in T = U_M^C$.

$T := U_M^C$

= A coherent system of units for the magnitudes M.

$1_S := 1_U$ = The unit element of U_M^C

The result is the definition of a particular model of an R-group, that justifies the standard rules governing the "symbolic" (nonarithmetic and theoretically nonjustified) products of numbers by units. We stipulate then

Definition 12. The structure

$N_M^C = \langle R, S, g, \bullet, \circ, ^{-1}, 1_U \rangle,$

with $f(R \times U_M^C)$,

is a coherent system of denominate numbers if and only if it is an R-group and if R is the field of real numbers and if

U_M^C

is a coherent system of units for some set M of magnitudes.

The foregoing nearly justifies writing '$P(a) = p\,u$' for the value of the magnitude P at the physical system a on the unit u. Not quite, because we have to do with two different functions: P and what we shall call its associated magnitude P'. More precisely, we stipulate the following definitions:

Definition 13. If $P: A \times B \times \rightarrow \times N \times U_p \rightarrow V$ is a magnitude concerning a complex of physical systems of the kinds A through N, then the *associated magnitude* is the function $P': A \times B \times \ldots \times N \rightarrow W$, where $W \subset S$ is a subset of the set of denominate numbers, such that

$P'(a, b, \ldots, n) = p\,u$ iff $P(a, b, \ldots, n, u) = p$.

Definition 14. The numerical value of $P: A \times B \times \ldots \times N \times U_p \rightarrow V$ at $a, b, \ldots, n, u$ with $a \in A$, $b \in B$, $\ldots$, $n \in N$ is called the *numeric* of P' for $\langle a, b, \ldots, n \rangle$.

The extension of the preceding definitions to vector valued and tensor valued functions is quite unnecessary, as they take care of every component.

Our axioms and definitions in this section sanction the otherwise lawless expressions of the form "*r u* ". They also dispel the popular belief that "3 cm" is of the same kind as "3 planets".

2.4 Species and Changes of Unit

The inch and the micron, though different, belong to the same set U_L. of length units, itself a subset of the totality U of units. We may thus write: in ~, where the relation ~ is an equivalence relation on U. More precisely, we lay down the following:

Definition 15. Given a magnitude P and its associated set U_p of units, any two members of this latter set are said to be *congruent*. In symbols,

If $u, u' \in U$, then: $u \sim u'$ iff $u, u' \in U_p \subset U$.

The name "congruence" for ~ has been chosen advisedly: ~ is in fact a congruence with respect to the multiplication of units. That is, if $u, u', v, v' \in U_p$, then:

If $u \sim u'$ and $v \sim v'$, then: $u \cdot v \sim u' \cdot v'$.

Since the relation of units congruence is an equivalence relation, it induces a partition of any set U into mutually disjoint equivalence classes, one per magnitude. Every such set is a species of units and the totality of such species, i.e. the quotient set $U / \sim$, may be called the *natural partition* of U. To be more explicit, we lay down the following:

Definition 16. If $u \in U$, the *species* of u is the ~ -equivalence class of u. In symbols,

$[u] = \{v \mid v \in U \text{ and } v \sim u\}$.

Caution: In the present context [ ] does not stand for the dimension function introduced in Section 1.5.

Definition 17. The quotient set $U / \sim$ is called the *family of species of units*.

Although U is a collection of individuals (units) and $U / \sim$ a family of sets (species of units) they have the same structure. Indeed, one can define an operation ? on the family of species of units as follows:

$[u] \rightarrow [v]$ = df $[u \cdot v]$.

This operation is associative. It is also well defined. Indeed, let u' $[u]$ and v' $[v]$. Then by the congruence property

$u' \cdot v \cdot [u \cdot v]$, i.e. $[u' \cdot v'] = [u \cdot v]$.

so that the operation does not depend on the choice of elements. Furthermore the unit element of the family of sets $U/\sim$ is $[1u] = \{1u\}$ since

$[u] \rightarrow [1_U] = [u \cdot 1_U] = [u]$.

Finally,

$[u]^{-1} = [u^{-1}]$

since

$[u] * [u^{-1}] = [u \cdot u^{-1}] = [1_U]$.

In short, we have proved.

Theorem 7. The structure $U/\sim \; = \; <U/\sim, *, ^{-1}, [1_u]>$, where $U/\sim$ is the quotient of a set U of units by the equivalence relation ? of same unit species, is an abelian group written multiplicatively.

We can now justify the customary rule governing unit conversions. The rule is based on following theorem:

Theorem 8. If $P: A \times B \times ... \times N \times U_p \rightarrow V$ is a magnitude and $u, u' \in U_p$, then the corresponding values of the associated magnitude P' for u are a linear transform of those for u':

$P'(a, b, \ldots, n) = p\,u = (\alpha\, p' + \beta)\, u'$, with $\alpha, \beta \in R$.

Example. u = centigrade degree, and u' = Fahrenheit degree, $\alpha = 5/9$, $\beta = -5.32/9$. In the vast majority of cases $\beta = 0$.

Corollary 1. If $u, u' \in U_p$ and $\beta = 0$, then the units ratio is a unit free real number, namely $u \cdot u^{-1} = p'/p$, called a *conversion factor.*

Corollary 2. The ratio of any two values of an associated magnitude is unit free, hence invariant under unit conversions, provided $\beta = 0$.

Units can be freely substituted as long as they are congruent, i.e. provided they belong to the same equivalence class. This substantiates the thesis, occasionally doubted, that *units are conventional*, hence devoid of physical content. (One cause for this doubt is a dislike of conventions for fear that they may lead to conventionalism a groundless fear no doubt. Another cause is the equally unjustified but widespread confusion of units with dimensions. A third is the confusion of units with standards. By the same token, the contention that units are dependent on, or even definable by, measurement is disproved. Rather on the contrary, most measurements presuppose the adoption of units. And, as shown by Axiom 5, such an adoption is an integral part of the choice of representation for physical quantities.

Since units are conventional, we are free to choose them not however capriciously but in accordance with theory and in the interests of expediency. To the former: (*a*) fundamental units should be units of physical quantities occurring as fundamental in some basic theory: thus we prefer to choose a fundamental unit of mass rather than weight because, as GAUSS noted, mechanics teaches us that mass is more fundamental and universal than weight; (*b*) all derivative units except the multiples and submultiples of fundamental units are built in accordance with some theoretical formulas. As to the expediency desideratum: although all of the coherent systems of units are rational, not all of them are reasonable or suitable for a given purpose. Some, e.g. the technical system, are cumbersome for theoretical work; others, e.g. the CGS system, are clumsy for practical purposes; finally others, particularly the various system of "natural" units, are devoid of heuristic value.

2.5 Units and Dimensions

Units and dimensions are clearly distinct even though they are often mixed up. Thus, while we can either postulate or compute *the* dimension of a physical quantity, we can only talk of *a* unit (or of a whole class of units) for the same quantity. In other words, whereas the physical quantity-dimension value relation is a function, the physical quantity-unit correspondence is a nonfunctional relation. (Only dimensionless physical quantities are unambiguous as far as units are concerned: they are all assigned the unit 1_U.) In rather obvious symbols: whereas $[P] = d$, where d is a dimension value, $\{P\} = U_p$. We shall presently clarify these ideas by exhibiting their formal relations. To this end we shall avail ourselves of a few results obtained in Section 1, where we introduced a distinction between the dimension function [ ] and the set D_Q of dimension values of a collection Q of physical quantities (magnitudes or dimensional constants). For our immediate purpose we only need to recall that [ ] is a certain function from a set Q of physical quantities to the set D_Q of associated dimension values.

Theorem 9. Let Q be a set of physical quantities and let $D_Q = <D_Q, \cdot, ^{-1}, 1_D>$ be the group of dimension values of Q. Further, let $U_Q / \sim$ be the family of all the species of units for Q. Then D_Q and $U / \sim$ are *isomorphic*, i.e. there exists a bijection

Ψ: $_{DQ} \to U_Q / \sim$.

Proof. By Theorem 7 in Section 2.4, $U/\sim$ is an abelian group. By Axiom 3 in Section 1.4, D_Q too is an abelian group. Moreover, for every physical quantity there is just one dimension value and just one species of units, so that the sets D_Q and $U/\sim$ are equally numerous. Finally, the operations are preserved: the products of dimension values are carried into products of units species, and similarly for the inverses. This proves the isomorphism between dimension values and species of units.

Now, every dimension value is in turn a physical quantity species, i.e. a member of the quotient of Q by the relation = of equidimensionality, as shown by Theorem 6 in Section 1.7. Hence the composition of the dimension function [ ] and the above isomorphism ø yields the sought functional relation { } between physical quantities and species of units, as exhibited by the commutative diagram

$$\begin{array}{ccc} Q & \rightarrow & D = Q/\equiv \\ & \{\,\}\searrow & \downarrow \varphi \\ & & U/\sim \end{array}$$

In other words, we have following theorem:

Theorem 10. Let Q be a set of physical quantities and let $U_Q/\sim$ be the corresponding family of units species. Further, let [ ] be the dimension function that maps Q into the set of dimension values of Q. Then the function $\{\}: Q \rightarrow U_Q/\sim$ such that $\{q\} = U_Q$ for every $q \in Q$, is the composition $\{\} = [\,] \circ \varphi$, where φ is the bijection between the dimension values and the units species.

This result elucidates the phrase "a unit of" with the help of the concept of dimension. Note that, on the other hand, the concept of dimension does not depend on the one of unit. This completes our mathematical study of units.

2.6 Units and Standards

Units are sometimes said to be defined by standards. Thus the metre is said to equal, by definition, the length of a certain body laying in state at Sevres. The corresponding statement is often called a *coordinative definition* following Reichenbach. But surely this constitutes an abuse of the word "definition" and it fails to elucidate the relations between units and standards.

There are two relations between units and standards, none of which is definitional. Firstly, whenever there happens to be a standard s for a given unit u in the set U_p of P-units, the unit (or rather the denominate number $1 \cdot u$) equals, to within measurement error, the measured value of the associated magnitude P' at the standard s:

Measured value of $P'(s) = (1 \pm)\, u$,

where σ is the standard deviation of the run of measurements concerned. For a sequence of ideally exact measurements, such as those imagined in the quantum theory of measurements, $\sigma = 0$ and consequently

Exact measured value of $P'(s) = P'(s) = 1 \cdot u$.

Secondly, whenever there is a standard, the corresponding unit may be said to equal, by *referition* (not definition), the *P*-ness of the given standard:

$1 \cdot U =_{rf} P'(s)$.

In either case s is a physical system and more particularly one belonging to the domain of the magnitude in question, whereas $1 \cdot u$ is a concept.

Therefore (*a*) the unit-standard relation cannot be definitional and (*b*) the criteria regulating the choice of standards need not be the same as those presiding over the choice of units. For one thing, technological considerations such as feasibility, stability, ease of replication, and cost, which are overriding in the case of standards, are totally irrelevant to the choice of a system of units, which is a theoretical problem. Standards are subject to natural law and to engineering design, and they must be regular and reliable. Units are subject to the algebra of units, they are part of a theoretical framework and they should be convenient. The confusion of units with standards is just an instance of the operationist tenet that every theoretical concept has got to be "defined" by reference to empirical operations.

2.7 Remarks on the Elucidation Procedure

Units have now ceased to be outcasts: they have been incorporated into the mathematical establishment. Likewise denominate numbers have ceased to be mere "symbolic" products to become charter members of a respectable mathematical structure, namely an *R*-group. Our characterization of the concept of a unit has not consisted in an explicit definition, let alone in a description of certain measurement procedures: the elucidation has been performed by a theory resting on a couple of postulates and containing, among others, two theorems relating units to dimensions. Consequently the answer to the question

"What is a unit?" is as precise as it is sibylline, namely this. A unit is whatever satisfies Axioms 5 and 6 above. Similarly with denominate numbers: a denominate number is an element of the *R*-group

$$N_M^C .$$

This clarification procedure (the axiomatic definition) is well known from mathematics and there is no other technique for elucidating basic (undefined) concepts, whether in mathematics or in physics.

❑❑❑

6

Quantum Mechanics: Theory and Implications

Introduction

Quantum mechanics (QM), also known as quantum physics or quantum theory, is a branch of physics providing a mathematical description of much of the dual particle-like and wave-like behaviour and interactions of energy and matter. It departs from classical mechanics primarily at the atomic and subatomic scales. In advanced topics of QM, some of these behaviors are macroscopic and only emerge at very low or very high energies or temperatures. The name, coined by Max Planck, derives from the observation that some physical quantities can be changed only by discrete amounts, or quanta, as multiples of the Planck constant, rather than being capable of varying continuously or by any arbitrary amount. For example, the angular momentum, or more generally the action, of an electron bound into an atom or molecule is quantized. An electron bound in an atomic orbital has quantized values of angular momentum while an unbound electron does not exhibit quantized energy levels. In the context of QM, the wave–particle duality of energy and matter and the uncertainty principle provide a unified view of the behaviour of photons, electrons and other atomic-scale objects.

The mathematical formulations of quantum mechanics are abstract and the implications are often non-intuitive in terms of classic physics. The centrepiece of the mathematical system is the wave function. The wave function is a mathematical function that can provide information about the probability amplitude of position and momentum of a particle. Mathematical manipulations of the wave function usually involve the bracket notation, which requires an understanding of complex numbers and linear functional. The wave function emphasizes the object as a quantum harmonic oscillator and the mathematics is akin to that of acoustics, resonance. Many of the results of QM do not have models that are easily visualized in terms of classical mechanics; for instance, the ground state in the quantum mechanical model is a non-zero energy state that is the lowest permitted energy state of a system, rather than a more traditional system that is thought of as simply being at rest with zero kinetic energy.

Historically, the earliest versions of QM were formulated in the first decade of the 20th century at around the same time as the atomic theory and the corpuscular theory of light as updated by Einstein first came to be widely accepted as scientific fact; these latter theories can be viewed as "quantum theories" of matter and electromagnetic radiation. QM underwent a significant re-formulation in the mid-1920's away from old quantum theory with the acceptance of the Copenhagen interpretation of Niels Bohr, Werner Heisenberg, Wolfgang Pauli and their associates. By 1930, QM had been further unified and formalized by the work of Paul Dirac and John von Neumann, with a greater emphasis placed on measurement in quantum mechanics, the statistical nature of our knowledge of reality and philosophical speculation about the role of the observer. QM has since branched out into almost every aspect of 20th century physics and other disciplines such as quantum chemistry, quantum electronics, quantum optics and quantum information science. Much of what might be considered 19th century physics has been re-evaluated as the classical limit of QM, and its more advanced developments in terms of quantum field theory and speculative quantum gravity theories.

History

The early history of quantum mechanics can be traced to the 1838 discovery of cathode rays by Michael Faraday. This was followed by the 1859 statement of the black body radiation problem by Gustav Kirchhoff, the 1877 suggestion by Ludwig Boltzmann that the energy states of a physical system can be discrete, and the 1900 quantum hypothesis of Max Planck. Planck's hypothesis that energy is radiated and absorbed in discrete "quanta," or "energy elements," enabled the correct derivation of the observed patterns of black body radiation. According to Planck, each energy element E is proportional to its frequency ν:

$$E = h\nu$$

where h is Planck's action constant. Planck insisted that this was simply an aspect of the processes of absorption and emission of radiation and had nothing to do with the physical reality of the radiation itself. However, in 1905 Albert Einstein interpreted Planck's quantum hypothesis realistically and used it to explain the photoelectric effect, in which shining light on certain materials can eject electrons from the material. Einstein postulated that light itself consists of individual quanta of energy, later called photons.

The foundations of quantum mechanics were established during the first half of the 20th century by Niels Bohr, Werner Heisenberg, Max Planck, Louis de Broglie, Albert Einstein,

Erwin Schrödinger, Max Born, John von Neumann, Paul Dirac, Wolfgang Pauli, David Hilbert, and others. In the mid-1920s, developments in quantum mechanics quickly led to its becoming the standard formulation for atomic physics. In the summer of 1925, Bohr and Heisenberg published results that closed the "Old Quantum Theory". Light quanta came to be called Photons (1926). From Einstein's simple postulation was born a flurry of debating, theorizing and testing, and thus the entire field of quantum physics emerged, leading to its wider acceptance at the Fifth Solvay Conference in 1927.

The other exemplar that led to quantum mechanics was the study of electromagnetic waves such as light. When it was found in 1900 by Max Planck that the energy of waves could be described as consisting of small packets or quanta, Albert Einstein further developed this idea to show that an electromagnetic wave such as light could be described by a particle called the photon with a discrete energy dependent on its frequency. This led to a theory of unity between subatomic particles and electromagnetic waves called wave–particle duality in which particles and waves were neither one nor the other, but had certain properties of both. While quantum mechanics describes the world of the very small, it also is needed to explain certain macroscopic quantum systems such as superconductors and superfluids.

The word *quantum* derives from Latin meaning "how great" or "how much". In quantum mechanics, it refers to a discrete unit that quantum theory assigns to certain physical quantities, such as the energy of an atom at rest. The discovery that particles are discrete packets of energy with wave-like properties led to the branch of physics that deals with atomic and subatomic systems which is today called quantum mechanics. It is the underlying mathematical framework of many fields of physics and chemistry, including condensed matter physics, solid-state physics, atomic physics, molecular physics, computational physics, computational chemistry, quantum chemistry, particle physics, nuclear chemistry and nuclear physics. Some fundamental aspects of the theory are still actively studied. Quantum mechanics is essential to understand the behaviour of systems at atomic length scales and smaller. For example, if classical mechanics governed the workings of an atom, electrons would rapidly travel towards and collide with the nucleus, making stable atoms impossible. However, in the natural world the electrons normally remain in an uncertain, non-deterministic "smeared" (wave–particle wave function) orbital path around or through the nucleus, defying classical electromagnetism. Quantum mechanics was initially developed to provide a better explanation of the atom, especially the spectra of light emitted by different atomic species. The quantum theory of the atom was developed as an explanation for the electron's staying in its orbital, which could not be explained by Newton's laws of motion and by Maxwell's laws of classical electromagnetism. Broadly speaking, quantum mechanics incorporates four classes of phenomena for which classical physics cannot account:

- The quantization (discretization) of certain physical quantities
- wave–particle duality
- uncertainty principle
- quantum entanglement

Mathematical Formulations

In the mathematically rigorous formulation of quantum mechanics, developed by Paul Dirac and John von Neumann, the possible states of a quantum mechanical system are represented by unit vectors (called "state vectors") residing in a complex separable Hilbert space (variously called the "state space" or the "associated Hilbert space" of the system) well defined up to a complex number of norm 1 (the phase factor). In other words, the possible states are points in the projectivization of a Hilbert space, usually called the complex projective space. The exact nature of this Hilbert space is dependent on the system; for example, the state space for position and momentum states is the space of square-integrable functions, while the state space for the spin of a single proton is just the product of two complex planes. Each observable is represented by a maximally Hermitian linear operator acting on the state space. Each eigen state of an observable corresponds to an eigenvector of the operator, and the associated eigenvalue corresponds to the value of the observable in that eigen state. If the operator's spectrum is discrete, the observable can only attain those discrete eigen values.

In the formalism of quantum mechanics, the state of a system at a given time is described by a complex wave function, also referred to as state vector in a complex vector space. This abstract mathematical object allows for the calculation of probabilities of outcomes of concrete experiments. For example, it allows one to compute the probability of finding an electron in a particular region around the nucleus at a particular time. Contrary to classical mechanics, one can never make simultaneous predictions of conjugate variables, such as position and momentum, with accuracy. For instance, electrons may be considered to be located somewhere within a region of space, but with their exact positions being unknown. Contours of constant probability, often referred to as "clouds", may be drawn around the nucleus of an atom to conceptualize where the electron might be located with the most probability. Heisenberg's uncertainty principle quantifies the inability to precisely locate the particle given its conjugate momentum.

As the result of a measurement, the wave function containing the probability information for a system collapses from a given initial state to a particular eigenstate of the observable. The possible results of a measurement are the eigenvalues of the operator representing the observable which explains the choice of *Hermitian* operators, for which all the eigenvalues are real. We can find the probability distribution of an observable in a given state by computing the spectral decomposition of the corresponding operator. Heisenberg's uncertainty principle is represented by the statement that the operators corresponding to certain observables do not commute.

The probabilistic nature of quantum mechanics thus stems from the act of measurement. This is one of the most difficult aspects of quantum systems to understand. It was the central topic in the famous Bohr-Einstein debates, in which the two scientists attempted to clarify these fundamental principles by way of thought experiments. In the decades after the formulation of quantum mechanics, the question of what constitutes a "measurement" has been extensively studied. Interpretations of quantum mechanics have been formulated to do away with the concept of "wave function collapse"; see, for example, the relative state interpretation. The basic idea is that when a quantum system interacts with a measuring apparatus, their respective wave functions become entangled, so that the original quantum system ceases to exist as an independent entity. For details, see the article on measurement in quantum mechanics. Generally, quantum mechanics does not assign definite values to observables. Instead, it makes predictions using probability distributions; that is, the probability of obtaining possible outcomes from measuring an observable. Often these results are skewed by many causes, such as dense probability clouds or quantum state nuclear attraction. Naturally, these probabilities will depend on the quantum state at the "instant" of the measurement. Hence, uncertainty is involved in the value. There are, however, certain states that are associated with a definite value of a particular observable. These are known as eigenstates of the observable.

In the everyday world, it is natural and intuitive to think of everything (every observable) as being in an eigenstate. Everything appears to have a definite position, a definite momentum, a definite energy, and a definite time of occurrence. However, quantum mechanics does not pinpoint the exact values of a particle for its position and momentum (since they are conjugate pairs) or its energy and time (since they too are conjugate pairs); rather, it only provides a range of probabilities of where that particle might be given its momentum and momentum probability. Therefore, it is helpful to use different words to describe states having uncertain values and states having definite values (eigenstate). Usually, a system will not be in an eigenstate of the observable we are interested in. However, if one measures the observable, the wavefunction will instantaneously be an eigenstate (or generalized eigenstate) of that observable. This process is known as wavefunction collapse, a debatable process. It involves expanding the system under study to include the measurement device. If one knows the corresponding wave function at the instant before the measurement, one will be able to compute the probability of collapsing into each of the possible eigenstates. For example, the free particle in the previous example will usually have a wavefunction that is a wave packet centered around some mean position x_0, neither an eigenstate of position nor of momentum. When one measures the position of the particle, it is impossible to predict with certainty the result. It is probable, but not certain, that it will be near x_0, where the amplitude of the wave function is large. After the measurement is performed, having obtained some result x, the wave function collapses into a position eigenstate centered at x.

The time evolution of a quantum state is described by the Schrödinger equation, in which the Hamiltonian, the operator corresponding to the total energy of the system, generates time evolution. The time evolution of wave functions is deterministic in the sense that, given a wavefunction at an initial time, it makes a definite prediction of what the wavefunction will be at any later time.

During a measurement, on the other hand, the change of the wavefunction into another one is not deterministic, but rather unpredictable, i.e., random. A time-evolution simulation can be seen here. Wave functions can change as time progresses. An equation known as the Schrödinger equation describes how wave functions change in time, a role similar to Newton's second law in classical mechanics. The Schrödinger equation, applied to the aforementioned example of the free particle, predicts that the centre of a wave packet will move through space at a constant velocity, like a classical particle with no forces acting on it. However, the wave packet will also spread out as time progresses, which means that the position becomes more uncertain. This also has the effect of turning position eigenstates (which can be thought of as infinitely sharp wave packets) into broadened wave packets that are no longer position eigenstates.

Some wave functions produce probability distributions that are constant, or independent of time, such as when in a stationary state of constant energy, time drops out of the absolute square of the wave function. Many systems that are treated dynamically in classical mechanics are described by such "static" wave functions. For example, a single electron in an unexcited atom is pictured classically as a particle moving in a circular trajectory around the atomic nucleus, whereas in quantum mechanics it is described by a static, spherically symmetric wavefunction surrounding the nucleus.

The Schrödinger equation acts on the entire probability amplitude, not merely its absolute value. Whereas the absolute value of the probability amplitude encodes information about probabilities, its phase encodes information about the interference between quantum states. This gives rise to the wave-like behavior of quantum states. It turns out that analytic solutions of Schrödinger's equation are only available for a small number of model Hamiltonians, of which the quantum harmonic oscillator, the particle in a box, the hydrogen molecular ion and the hydrogen atom are the most important representatives. Even the helium atom, which contains just one more electron than hydrogen, defies all attempts at a fully analytic treatment. There exist several techniques for generating approximate solutions. For instance, in the method known as perturbation theory one uses the analytic results for a simple quantum mechanical model to generate results for a more complicated model related to the simple model by, for example, the addition of a weak potential energy. Another method is the "semi-classical equation of motion" approach, which applies to systems for which quantum mechanics produces weak deviations from classical behavior. The deviations can be calculated based on the classical motion. This approach is important for the field of quantum chaos.

There are numerous mathematically equivalent formulations of quantum mechanics. One of the oldest and most commonly used formulations is the transformation theory proposed by Cambridge theoretical physicist Paul Dirac, which unifies and generalizes the two earliest formulations of quantum mechanics, matrix mechanics (invented by Werner Heisenberg) and wave mechanics (invented by Erwin Schrödinger). In this formulation, the instantaneous state of a quantum system encodes the probabilities of its measurable properties, or "observables". Examples of observables include energy, position, momentum, and angular momentum. Observables can be either continuous (e.g., the position of a particle) or discrete (e.g., the energy of an electron bound to a hydrogen atom). An alternative formulation of quantum mechanics is Feynman's path integral formulation, in which a quantum-mechanical amplitude is considered as a sum over histories between initial and final states; this is the quantum-mechanical counterpart of action principles in classical mechanics.

Interactions with Other Scientific Theories

The fundamental rules of quantum mechanics are very deep. They assert that the state space of a system is a Hilbert space and the observables are Hermitian operators acting on that space, but do not tell us which Hilbert space or which operators, or if it even exists. These must be chosen appropriately in order to obtain a quantitative description of a quantum system. An important guide for making these choices is the correspondence principle, which states that the predictions of quantum mechanics reduce to those of classical physics when a system moves to higher energies or equivalently, larger quantum numbers. In other words, classical mechanics is simply a quantum mechanics of large systems. This "high energy" limit is known as the *classical* or *correspondence limit*. One can therefore start from an established classical model of a particular system, and attempt to guess the underlying quantum model that gives rise to the classical model in the correspondence limit.

When quantum mechanics was originally formulated, it was applied to models whose correspondence limit was non-relativistic classical mechanics. For instance, the well-known model of the quantum harmonic oscillator uses an explicitly non-relativistic expression for the kinetic energy of the oscillator, and is thus a quantum version of the classical harmonic oscillator.

Early attempts to merge quantum mechanics with special relativity involved the replacement of the Schrödinger equation with a covariant equation such as the Klein-Gordon equation or the Dirac equation. While these theories were successful in explaining many experimental results, they had certain unsatisfactory qualities stemming from their neglect of the relativistic creation and annihilation of particles. A fully relativistic quantum theory required the development of quantum field theory, which applies quantization to a field rather than a fixed set of particles. The first complete quantum field theory, quantum electrodynamics, provides a fully quantum description of the electromagnetic interaction. The full apparatus of quantum field theory is often unnecessary for describing electrodynamic systems. A simpler approach, one employed since the inception of quantum mechanics, is to treat charged particles as quantum mechanical objects being acted on by a classical electromagnetic field. For example, the elementary quantum model of the hydrogen atom describes the electric field of the hydrogen atom using a classical $-\frac{e^2}{4\pi\,^{\epsilon}0\tau}$ Coulomb potential. This "semi-classical" approach fails if quantum fluctuations in the electromagnetic field play an important role, such as in the emission of photons by charged particles. Quantum field theories for the strong nuclear force and the weak nuclear force have been developed. The quantum field theory of the strong nuclear force is called quantum chromodynamics, and describes the interactions of the subnuclear particles: quarks and gluons. The weak nuclear force and the electromagnetic force were unified, in their quantized forms, into a single quantum field theory known as electroweak theory, by the physicists Abdus Salam, Sheldon Glashow and Steven Weinberg. These three men shared the Nobel Prize in Physics in 1979 for this work.

It has proven difficult to construct quantum models of gravity, the remaining fundamental force. Semi-classical approximations are workable, and have led to predictions such as Hawking radiation. However, the formulation of a complete theory of quantum gravity is hindered by apparent incompatibilities between general relativity, the most accurate theory of gravity currently known, and some of the fundamental assumptions of quantum theory. The resolution of these incompatibilities is an area of active research, and theories such as string theory are among the possible candidates for a future theory of quantum gravity. Classical mechanics has been extended into the complex domain and complex classical mechanics exhibits behaviours similar to quantum mechanics.

Quantum Mechanics and Classical Physics

Predictions of quantum mechanics have been verified experimentally to a very high degree of accuracy. According to the correspondence principle between classical and quantum mechanics, all objects obey the laws of quantum mechanics, and classical mechanics is just an approximation for large systems (or a statistical quantum mechanics of a large collection of particles). The laws of classical mechanics thus follow from the laws of quantum mechanics as a statistical average at the limit of large systems or large quantum numbers. However, chaotic systems do not have good quantum numbers, and quantum chaos studies the relationship between classical and quantum descriptions in these systems.

Quantum coherence is an essential difference between classical and quantum theories, and is illustrated by the Einstein-Podolsky-Rosen paradox. Quantum interference involves the addition of *probability amplitudes*, whereas when classical waves interfere there is an addition of intensities. For microscopic bodies, the extension of the system is much smaller than the coherence length, which gives rise to long-range entanglement and other nonlocal phenomena characteristic of quantum systems. Quantum coherence is not typically evident at macroscopic scales, although an exception to this rule can occur at extremely low temperatures, when quantum behaviour can manifest itself on more macroscopic scales. This is in accordance with the following observations:

- Many macroscopic properties of a classical system are a direct consequences of the quantum behavior of its parts. For example, the stability of bulk matter (which consists of atoms and molecules which would quickly collapse under electric forces alone), the rigidity of solids, and the mechanical, thermal, chemical, optical and magnetic properties of matter are all results of the interaction of electric charges under the rules of quantum mechanics.

- While the seemingly exotic behaviour of matter posited by quantum mechanics and relativity theory become more apparent when dealing with extremely fast-moving or extremely tiny particles, the laws of classical Newtonian physics remain accurate in predicting the behaviour of large objects of the order of the size of large molecules and bigger at velocities much smaller than the velocity of light.

Relativity and Quantum Mechanics

Even with the defining postulates of both Einstein's theory of general relativity and quantum theory being indisputably supported by rigorous and repeated empirical evidence and while they do not directly contradict each other theoretically (at least with regard to primary claims), they are resistant to being incorporated within one cohesive model.

Einstein himself is well known for rejecting some of the claims of quantum mechanics. While clearly contributing to the field, he did not accept the more philosophical consequences and interpretations of quantum mechanics, such as the lack of deterministic causality and the assertion that a single subatomic particle can occupy numerous areas of space at one time. He also was the first to notice some of the apparently exotic consequences of entanglement and used them to formulate the Einstein-Podolsky-Rosen paradox, in the hope of showing that quantum mechanics had unacceptable implications. This was 1935, but in 1964 it was shown by John Bell that, although Einstein was correct in identifying seemingly paradoxical implications of quantum mechanical nonlocality, these implications could be experimentally tested. Alain Aspect's initial experiments in 1982, and many subsequent experiment since, have verified quantum entanglement.

According to the paper of J. Bell and the Copenhagen interpretation (the common interpretation of quantum mechanics by physicists since 1927), and contrary to Einstein's ideas, quantum mechanics was not at the same time

- a "realistic" theory
- and a *local* theory

The Einstein-Podolsky-Rosen paradox shows in any case that there exist experiments by which one can measure the state of one particle and instantaneously change the state of its entangled partner, although the two particles can be an arbitrary distance apart; however, this effect does not violate causality, since no transfer of information happens. Quantum entanglement is at the basis of quantum cryptography, with high-security commercial applications in banking and government.

Gravity is negligible in many areas of particle physics, so that unification between general relativity and quantum mechanics is not an urgent issue in those applications. However, the lack of a correct theory of quantum gravity is an important issue in cosmology and physicists' search for an elegant "theory of everything". Thus, resolving the inconsistencies between both theories has been a major goal of twentieth- and twenty-first-century physics. Many prominent physicists, including Stephen Hawking, have labored in the attempt to discover a theory underlying *everything*, combining not only different models of subatomic physics, but also deriving the universe's four forces the strong force, electromagnetism, weak force, and gravity from a single force or phenomenon. One of the leaders in this field is Edward Witten, a theoretical physicist who formulated the groundbreaking M-theory, which is an attempt at describing the supersymmetrical based string theory.

Attempts at a Unified Field Theory

As of 2010 the quest for unifying the fundamental forces through quantum mechanics is still ongoing. Quantum electrodynamics (or "quantum electromagnetism"), which is currently (in the perturbative regime at least) the most accurately tested physical theory, has been successfully merged with the weak nuclear force into the electroweak force and work is currently being done to merge the electroweak and strong force into the electrostrong force. Current predictions state that at around 10^{14} GeV the three aforementioned forces are fused into a single unified field, Beyond this "grand unification," it is speculated that it may be possible to merge gravity with the other three gauge symmetries, expected to occur at roughly 10^{19} GeV. However and while special relativity is parsimoniously incorporated into quantum electrodynamics the expanded general relativity, currently the best theory describing the gravitation force, has not been fully incorporated into quantum theory.

Philosophical Implications

Since its inception, the many counter-intuitive results of quantum mechanics have provoked strong philosophical debate and many interpretations. Even fundamental issues such as Max Born's basic rules concerning probability amplitudes and probability distributions took decades to be appreciated.

The Copenhagen interpretation, due largely to the Danish theoretical physicist Niels Bohr, is the interpretation of the quantum mechanical formalism most widely accepted amongst physicists. According to it, the probabilistic nature of quantum mechanics is not a temporary feature which will eventually be replaced by a deterministic theory, but instead must be considered to be a final renunciation of the classical ideal of causality. In this interpretation, it is believed that any well-defined application of the quantum mechanical formalism must always make reference to the experimental arrangement, due to the complementarity nature of evidence obtained under different experimental situations.

Albert Einstein, himself one of the founders of quantum theory, disliked this loss of determinism in measurement. (This dislike is the source of his famous quote, "God does not play dice with the universe.") Einstein held that there should be a local hidden variable theory underlying quantum mechanics and that, consequently, the present theory was incomplete. He produced a series of objections to the theory, the most famous of which has become known as the Einstein-Podolsky-Rosen paradox. John Bell showed that the EPR paradox led to experimentally testable differences between quantum mechanics and local realistic theories. Experiments have been performed confirming the accuracy of quantum mechanics, thus demonstrating that the physical world cannot be described by local realistic theories. The Bohr-Einstein debates provide a vibrant critique of the Copenhagen Interpretation from an epistemological point of view.

The Everett many-worlds interpretation, formulated in 1956, holds that all the possibilities described by quantum theory simultaneously occur in a multiverse composed of mostly independent parallel universes. This is not accomplished by introducing some new axiom to quantum mechanics, but on the contrary by removing the axiom of the collapse of the wave packet: All the possible consistent states of the measured system and the measuring apparatus (including the observer) are present in a real physical (not just formally mathematical, as in other interpretations) quantum superposition. Such a superposition of consistent state combinations of different systems is called an entangled state. While the multiverse is deterministic, we perceive non-deterministic behaviour governed by probabilities, because we can observe only the universe, i.e. the consistent state contribution to the mentioned superposition, we inhabit. Everett's interpretation is perfectly consistent with John Bell's experiments and makes them intuitively understandable. However, according to the theory of quantum decoherence, the parallel universes will never be accessible to us. This inaccessibility can be understood as follows: Once a measurement is done, the measured system becomes entangled with both the physicist who measured it and a huge number of other particles, some of which are photons flying away towards the other end of the universe; in order to prove that the wave function did not collapse one would have to bring all these particles back and measure them again, together with the system that was measured originally. This is completely impractical, but even if one could theoretically do this, it would destroy any evidence that the original measurement took place (including the physicist's memory).

Applications

Quantum mechanics had enormous success in explaining many of the features of our world. The individual behaviour of the subatomic particles that make up all forms of matter electrons, protons, neutrons, photons and others can often only be satisfactorily described using quantum mechanics. Quantum mechanics has strongly influenced string theory, a candidate for a theory of everything and the multiverse hypothesis.

Quantum mechanics is important for understanding how individual atoms combine covalently to form chemicals or molecules. The application of quantum mechanics to chemistry is known as quantum chemistry. (Relativistic) quantum mechanics can in principle mathematically describe most of chemistry. Quantum mechanics can provide quantitative insight into ionic and covalent bonding processes by explicitly showing which molecules are energetically favorable to which others, and by approximately how much. Most of the calculations performed in computational chemistry rely on quantum mechanics.

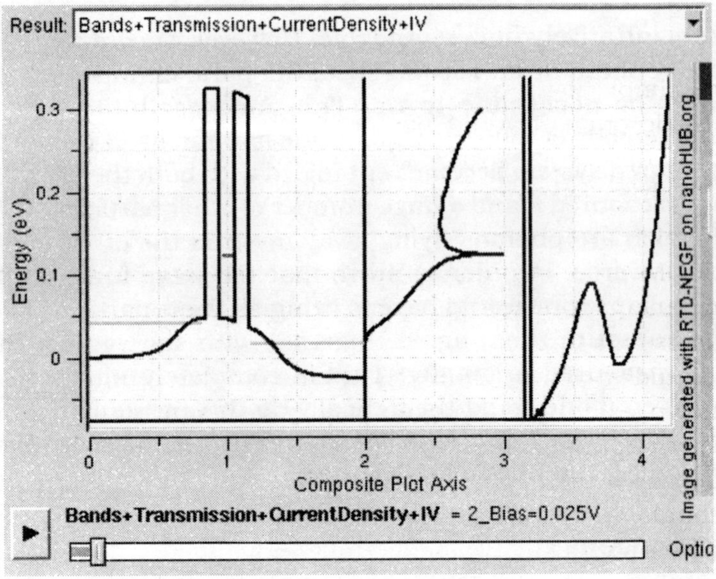

A working mechanism of a resonant tunneling diode device, based on the phenomenon of quantum tunneling through the potential barriers.

Much of modern technology operates at a scale where quantum effects are significant. Examples include the laser, the transistor (and thus the microchip), the electron microscope, and magnetic resonance imaging. The study of semiconductors led to the invention of the diode and the transistor, which are indispensable for modern electronics.

Researchers are currently seeking robust methods of directly manipulating quantum states. Efforts are being made to develop quantum cryptography, which will allow guaranteed secure transmission of information. A more distant goal is the development of quantum computers, which are expected to perform certain computational tasks exponentially faster than classical computers. Another active research topic is quantum teleportation, which deals with techniques to transmit quantum information over arbitrary distances.

Quantum tunneling is vital in many devices, even in the simple light switch, as otherwise the electrons in the electric current could not penetrate the potential barrier made up of a layer of oxide. Flash memory chips found in USB drives use quantum tunneling to erase their memory cells.

QM primarily applies to the atomic regimes of matter and energy, but some systems exhibit quantum mechanical effects on a large scale; superfluidity (the frictionless flow of a liquid at temperatures near absolute zero) is one well-known example. Quantum theory also provides accurate descriptions for many previously unexplained phenomena such as black body radiation and the stability of electron orbitals. It has also given insight into the workings of many different biological systems, including smell receptors and protein structures. Recent work on photosynthesis has provided evidence that quantum correlations play an essential role in this most fundamental process of the plant kingdom. Even so, classical physics often can be a good approximation to results otherwise obtained by quantum physics, typically in circumstances with large numbers of particles or large quantum numbers.

Examples

Particle in a Box

The particle in a 1-dimensional potential energy box is the most simple example where restraints lead to the quantization of energy levels. The box is defined as having zero potential energy inside a certain region and infinite potential energy everywhere outside that region. For the 1-dimensional case in the x direction, the time-independent Schrodinger equation can be written as:

$$-\frac{\hbar^2}{2m}\frac{d^2\psi}{dx^2} = E\psi$$

Writing the differential operator

$$\hat{p}_x = -i\hbar \frac{d}{dx}$$

the previous equation can be seen to be evocative of the classic analogue

$$\frac{1}{2m} \hat{p}_x^2 = E$$

with E as the energy for the state Ψ, in this case coinciding with the kinetic energy of the particle.

The general solutions of the Schrödinger equation for the particle in a box are:

$$\psi(x) = Ae^{ikx} + Be^{-ikx} \qquad E = \frac{\hbar^2 k^2}{2m}$$

or, from Euler's formula,

$$\psi(x) = C \sin kx + D \cos kx.$$

The presence of the walls of the box determines the values of C, D, and k. At each wall ($x = 0$ and $x = L$), $\psi = 0$. Thus when $x = 0$,

$$\psi(0) = 0 = C \sin 0 + D \cos 0 = D$$

and so $D = 0$. When $x = L$,

$$\psi(L) = 0 = C \sin kL.$$

C cannot be zero, since this would conflict with the Born interpretation. Therefore $\sin kL = 0$, and so it must be that kL is an integer multiple of π. Therefore,

$$k = \frac{n\pi}{L} \qquad n = 1, 2, 3, \ldots$$

The quantization of energy levels follows from this constraint on k, since

$$E = \frac{\hbar^2 \pi^2 n^2}{2mL^2} = \frac{n^2 h^2}{8mL^2}.$$

Free Particle

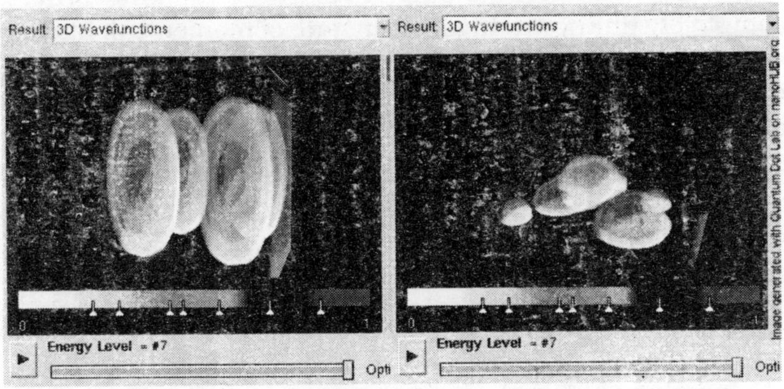

3D confined electron wave functions for each eigenstate in a Quantum Dot. Here, rectangular and triangular-shaped quantum dots are shown. Energy states in rectangular dots are more '*s*-type' and '*p*-type'. However, in a triangular dot the wave functions are mixed due to confinement symmetry.

For example, consider a free particle. In quantum mechanics, there is wave-particle duality so the properties of the particle can be described as the properties of a wave. Therefore, its quantum state can be represented as a wave of arbitrary shape and extending over space as a wave function. The position and momentum of the particle are observables. The Uncertainty Principle states that both the position and the momentum cannot simultaneously be measured with full precision at the same time. However, one can measure the position alone of a moving free particle creating an eigenstate of position with a wavefunction that is very large (a Dirac delta) at a particular position x and zero everywhere else. If one performs a position measurement on such a wavefunction, the result x will be obtained with 100% probability (full certainty). This is called an eigenstate of position (mathematically more precise: a *generalized position eigenstate (eigendistribution)*). If the particle is in an eigenstate of position then its momentum is completely unknown. On the other hand, if the particle is in an eigenstate of momentum then its position is completely unknown. In an eigenstate of momentum having a plane wave form, it can be shown that the wavelength is equal to h/p, where h is Planck's constant and p is the momentum of the eigenstate.

7

Light and Waves

Introduction

"Light" is not only that by means of which we see; and the infinitely precious layer of peculiar cells at the back of the human eye, the health of which makes all the difference for us between sight and perpetual darkness, is at its best perpetually blind to all but a very small fraction of the light waves which envelop and assail us. Most people are aware by now of some of these "invisible" rays, but are not yet experienced in thinking of them as light. There are the rays which are the cause of sunburn and yet are not a part of the sunlight perceived by the eye, since a windowpane intercepts them without making the sun seem any less bright. There are the rays which an X-ray tube emits, pernicious usually but capable of being helpful when intelligently managed, like a deadly poison which becomes a medicine when wisely used. There are the waves which radiate from electrical circuits having currents flowing in them and are detected through the currents which they cause to flow in other circuits: anyone who listens to a broadcast is making use of these.

These all, and many more, are types of light each occupying its particular place in that far-reaching roster or gamut which is called the "spectrum," where the prismatic colours also have their own small part. Any large physical laboratory is full of substitutes for eyes, each designed for responding to some range of the spectrum to which our natural instrument of sight is unresponsive. Most of them, apart from the electrical circuits responding to radio waves, are photographic plates of many sorts; but there are other types of very diverse nature, and even the Wilson chamber may be accounted as one. Most of what we know about the structure of atoms has been learned by studying light; and of this, the major part is due to the waves which only these eye-substitutes perceive. Had we to reply on our eyes exclusively, we should find it as hard to make out the organization of.

This huge extension of the spectrum beyond the range of eyesight began to be known at a date very easy to remember, the year 1800. It was then already more than one hundred and thirty years since Newton had dispersed the light of the sun with a prism and had resolved it thus into what we still call the prismatic or spectral colours, ranging from violet to red. The beam of white sunlight is spread out into a fanwise broadening beam of the several spectral colours side by side.

This is the separation or unmixing of white light into its coloured components; but it is also much more. In 1800 the English astronomer Herschel took a thermometer with blackened bulb, and moved it across the fan shaped beam. He observed that it grew steadily warmer as it passed from the violet toward and into the red; and then, he pushed it clear out of the fan and into the darkness beyond the red and observed that, instead of ceasing forthwith to respond, it became even hotter! Invisible rays beyond the red were accompanying the parti coloured beam: the prism had sifted out of the sunlight a component unable to stir the eye to response, yet capable of producing heat in something upon which it fell

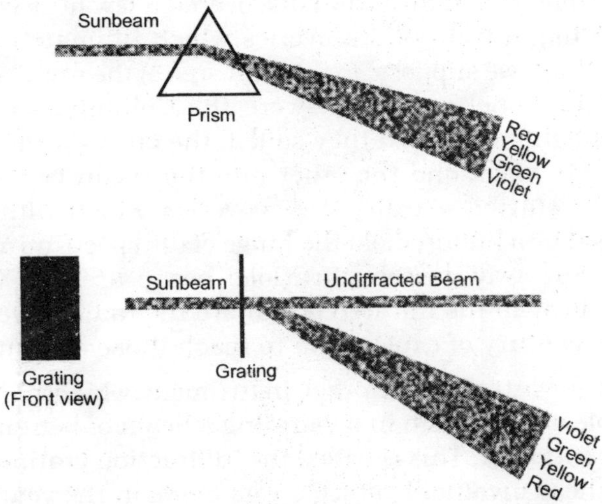

Figure 7.1. Illustrating the dispersion of white light into its spectrum by a prism and by a wire grating

(and therefore, we now say, laden with energy). In the very next year, the German chemist Ritter took what now would be called an extremely primitive type of photographic plate. This instrument he moved across the fan-shaped beam, and he observed that it began to react as, coming from the red side, it entered into the violet; and then, he shifted it clear out of the beam and into the darkness beyond the violet and observed that the reaction, instead of ceasing forthwith, became even stronger. Invisible rays beyond the violet were accompanying the parti-coloured beam: the prism had sifted out of the sunlight a component to which a photographic plate is sensitive, but not the eye.

Probably at the time of these discoveries, it must have seemed as though these invisible rays were only minor extensions of the fan-shaped beam embracing the visible spectrum from violet to red. But as the years went by, the process of extending the extensions went on and on and on, until the visible spectrum itself became the minor part and finally shrank to a small subdivision. Columbus, when he set sail upon the Atlantic and discovered a few little islands, was starting a train of discoveries which ultimately added about a third, we suppose, to the land area of the world already known. Herschel and Ritter were the Columbuses of the world of light; and when they sailed, the one into the ocean beyond the violet and the other into the ocean beyond the red, they started a train of discoveries which ultimately multiplied by a hundredfold the range of the spectrum already known. Far away in the ultraviolet ocean are the X-rays, and far away in the infrared ocean are the radio waves; but it took a century of exploration to reach those distant seas.

Now we introduce another instrument which plays the same role as the prism in separating a beam of light into its component parts. This is called the "diffraction grating." The first of these invaluable objects was made in the year 1820 by Fraunhofer, a native of Munich who as a lad was a glazier's apprentice and was given scope for his genius by a unique experience. "Unique," of course, is a dangerous word to employ; but I doubt whether anyone else has ever owed a distinguished career to the fact that his house fell down on him. Literally this happened to Fraunhofer. Other people lay dead in the ruins, but some of the beams leaned over in such a way as to shelter the boy in a cavity, and after five hours he was safely removed. A great crowd came to witness the rescue, among them the elector of Bavaria, and a man who was the head of what would now be called a scientific-instrument company; the monarch gave money to the boy, and later the other man, noting what Fraunhofer did with the money (he bought himself free of the apprenticeship and tried to start a lens-grinding business), gave him first a job and then a partnership; this by the way makes Fraunhofer one of the line, perhaps the first of the line, of industrial physicists.

Fraunhofer's earliest grating was of a type no longer used, but it serves as well as any for my exposition. It was simply a comb or ladder of parallel wires with gaps between them identical wires and exactly equal gaps. It is greatly magnified in the sketch, for actually there must be hundreds of wires to the inch. If now one projects a beam of sunlight against the comb from the side, it traverses the comb and emerges as a fanshaped beam, exhibiting the prismatic colours and accompanied on either side by the invisible rays of which I have been speaking. *The grating treats the light as would a prism,* dispersing a beam and separating its components. The analogy is not perfect—there are differences in detail: for instance, grating and prism disperse the colours in opposite order, so that now the violet is the least-deflected and the red the most-deflected hue of the visible spectrum. Such details are not important to us now; both devices are capable of sifting out the various components of a light-beam, and this is all that matters. The reason for discarding the prism is that its mode of action depends upon the molecules inside the glass and is complicated and obscure, whereas the grating is intelligible. It is in fact the grating which requires the wave theory of light, which proves the wave theory of light and which enables us to determine the wave lengths of light. This statement merits repetition and italics: *the action of the grating is what requires the wave theory of light, what proves the wave theory of light, and what enables us to determine wave lengths of light.* Other instruments possess these features, but it is the grating which exhibits them most clearly. To show how a grating treats waves, I insert a sequence of pictures.

Here is a wave: not a light-wave, of course, but a wave of sound. It is not a member of a train of waves, such as we shall hereafter be considering: it is just one wave or wave crest all by itself. Some would prefer to call it a pulse, but we think there will be no harm in calling it just one wave. You will guess that it represents a very sharp, sudden, and violent sound; and so it does to wit, the crack of an electric spark. The spark was behind the black blob in the centre of the picture, which was put there in order to prevent its light from spoiling the plate before the picture should be taken. The picture was taken a small fraction of a second after the spark, when the wave was still out in the open and had not impinged on anything much except the rear wall, from which as you see a part of it has been reflected. The next picture was taken a small fraction of a second later yet. By this time, evidently, the wave has got into trouble. We are, however, interested only in one feature of its troubles. Notice that every time it passed over one of the steps of the staircase a new wave sprang from the step and spread forth into the air. This new wave is feebler by far than the big one, so I will call it a "wavelet." Here is illustrated the first principle of a wave motion; whenever a wave on its way through space meets an irregularity of any kind an obstacle, a salient, a corner, a projection it generates a wavelet, which starts a new career of its own from the scene of the irregularity.

Here is a pulse on its way toward a very unpleasant-looking ceiling punctured with large holes. One might think that a hole, of all things, would not inspire a wave to produce a wavelet, but we choose the word "irregularity" just so as to include such cases as this one. Next is what happens after the wave hits the ceiling; you see that each of the holes has indeed become the centre of a wavelet, and you see also that these wavelets are by way of merging themselves into a new wave, which is starting back along the course of the original wave and is in fact predestined to be the wave reflected from the ceiling. This reflected wave does not look nearly so smooth and neat as the waves reflected from the smooth walls at the sides; and yet even these last are themselves composed of tiny wavelets of the invisibly feeble wavelets which have sprung from the individual atoms of the walls. Here, then, is the second principle. When a wave runs into a great number of obstacles or a great number of irregularities side by side, a wavelet springs from every one of them; and these wavelets may recombine themselves into a new wave, a sort of resurrection of the old one which was so badly lacerated; and this new wave may go off in a different direction from the old one.

For the third principle; I show another sketch. Here is the grating again in profile, and to the left of it four lines which we mean to represent four pulses following one another along at equal intervals and approaching the grating. (Please disregard, for the present, the snaky curve which intersects them.) On the right is a very crude approximation of what is going on perhaps a millionth of a second later, after the pulses have crashed into the grating. Each of the wires has become the centre of four consecutive wavelets, which are marching along one after the other. Clearly, the wavelets due to the first of the waves are already engaged in reconstituting that wave, and likewise those due to the second wave and those which are due to the third and the fourth. We have not drawn these wavelets as complete semicircles, though that would be the wisest policy if it did not entail so much crisscrossing of the curves as to make the drawing difficult to grasp. Now comes the cardinal point.

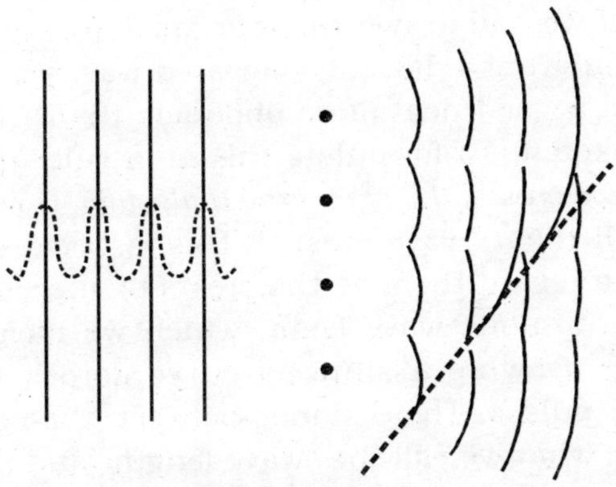

Figure 7.2. Illustrating how wavelets merge to form a diffracted wave front.

Notice the oblique line drawn tangent to four wavelets proceeding from four consecutive wires and due to four consecutive pulses. It looks as though it were meant for a wave itself, and that is precisely its meaning: the four wavelets in question *are* able to merge and coalesce into an obliquely directed wave, outspread along the line of this tangent. Not the whole of their energy, of course, is so directed, for otherwise there would be no light continuing straight onward; but some of the energy of these wavelets actually apportions itself in such a way.

This obliquely directed wave, traveling along in the direction normal to the tangent line, and therefore getting farther and farther away from the straight-onward path of the undeflected pulses as it proceeds—this *is what is technically called a "diffracted wave."* Perhaps it will be more picturesque if I call it a "staggered wave," as it is built up by picking out staggered members from the processions of wavelets that originate from each of the wires. Henceforth we shall consider only these staggered or diffracted waves, and those which go straight forward in the original direction of the beam will concern us no longer.

Now, a fairly obvious rule about these diffracted waves. Notice that if we had drawn the four oncoming pulses, say twice as far apart as I did, the staggered waves would have been slanted a good deal more obliquely than they are in the actual sketch. To formulate this as a rule: *the farther apart the wave crests, the bigger the deflection.* Now we have begun to call them "wave crests." This is because we are henceforth to regard them as the crests of successive hills of a long continuous wave train, which we have already indicated by drawing a sinuous curve across the lines denoting the pulses. The distance between the crests of a wave train is what we call the "wave length" and denote by the Greek letter » (read *lambda*): therefore, *the greater the wave length the greater the deflection.*

The red light has the longest waves of all the visible colours, the violet light the shortest; the ultraviolet has shorter waves than any visible light, the infrared has the longest waves of all. Each wave length is diffracted in a particular direction, so that we have only to measure the angle at which a given kind of light goes off and then tell off its wave length, by a formula which I refrain from quoting as it involves a trigonometric function.

To speak of wave trains suggests a railroad simile. The grating is a switchman who sees all the wave trains coming along a common track and switches each one of them aside, each to a particular diverging track of its own according to its wave length. He is a very wonderful switchman indeed, or perhaps we should say that the trains are wonderful; for even when a limitless number of trains are all arriving together, he is not bothered in the least; he sends them simultaneously on their separate ways, and they cross one another freely and depart without ever a collision or a derailment or a smashup. This, then, is the dispersion of light by a grating: the switching of all the wave trains of the oncoming mixture, each safely and smoothly onto its separate path.

I have tried to suggest all this by a sketch (Figure 7.3), where a mixture of wave trains impinges on the grating from the left, and its component trains go off in various directions on the right; but alas, all such attempts at picturing are so weak that one fears they are more dangerous than helpful. In looking at this sketch, pray do not think that the oncoming beam from the left is so narrow that it impinges on one wire only! it is broad enough to overlap hundreds or thousands of parallel wires at once. All the space to the left of the grating is filled with oscillation, as the water of a stormy sea is filled with undulation to a depth of many feet below its surface; and on the right, the diverging beams of the various wave lengths do not disentangle and separate themselves completely and go alone on their several ways until they are much farther away from the grating than my drawing suggests. Also from most sources of light, the sun in particular, there emanate very many more different wave lengths of light than appear in the picture.

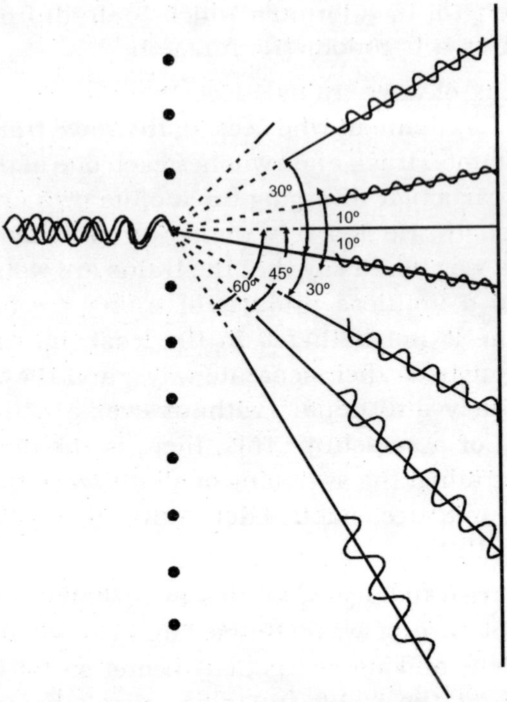

Figure 7.3. A mixture of wave trains of various wave lengths diffracted by a wire grating.

It is obvious, we suppose, that we are implying that the dispersion of a beam of light sunlight, for example-into diverging rays by a grating is proof that the light consists of wave trains. But one might begin to argue as follows: granted that the sunbeam is divided into rays of violet and yellow and red shooting off at various angles, why not just suppose that there are corpuscles of violet light and corpuscles of yellow light and corpuscles of red light all mixed up together in the sunbeam, and that when they hit the wires of the grating they simply bounce off sidewise, each at its own peculiar angle?

Well, in the first place it would be a very singular law of bouncing which we should have to postulate; and in the second place, one would certainly expect the angles of deviation to depend on such things as the shape, the thickness, and the material of the wires, and this they do *not*—not in the least. Perhaps these difficulties could somehow be evaded, but not the greatest one of all, which may be exemplified thus. You will readily see that the staggered wave will be wheeled around very considerably, and its course will be deflected from that of the oncoming sunbeam by a notably greater amount. Diminishing the spacing *d* between the wires of the grating, without changing the wires themselves in the least, is a way of increasing the deviation of every wave train increasing these deviations according to a law, which is easy to derive but which again we do not quote because it is trigonometric in form.

Now, when gratings of different spacing are presented to a sunbeam, the deviations of the different coloured rays do vary according to this law; and this is the fact which dominates everything. If it were just a case of corpuscles bouncing off the wires, then surely it should make no difference to the corpuscles whether the wires are spaced at five hundred to the inch or at one thousand to the inch! In the latter case twice as many might have the chance of bouncing as in the former, but those which bounced at all would bounce in the same direction. To put it more crisply: if a beam of, say, violet light is just a stream of corpuscles, its deflection at the grating should depend only on the shape of the individual wires and not on their spacing, since the corpuscle which hits a particular wire has dealings only with that one and does not know how far away the others are; while if it is just a train of waves, its deflection at the grating should depend on the spacing between the wires, and depend on it according to that law which we just mentioned. It is the latter alternative which is the truth; and this is the reason for accepting the wave theory of light. If anyhow we require the corpuscles just the same But now we are infringing on the topic of the chapter following, which will be full enough of intellectual troubles.

As I have intimated, the angle of deflection of a given kind of light of a specific, sharply definite wave length, "monochromatic" light as we say does not depend on the shape or the nature of the wire; and this is a principle giving great freedom in design. One may replace the ladder of wires by a sheet of gold leaf on glass, dividing the gold into narrow parallel strips of equal width and peeling off alternate strips; or use a diamond for scratching parallel lines upon the glass itself, the scratches now playing the role of the wires and the strips of smooth glass between them taking over the part of the gaps between the wires; or scratch the parallel lines or "rulings" upon the smoothed-off surface of a block of metal. Fraunhofer himself progressed through all these stages, and the world has followed chiefly the last of his examples. Light cannot, of course, come through a solid block of metal from behind; the beam falls slantingly upon the furrowed surface from the front, and a part of its energy is reflected according to the usual manner of reflection from a perfect mirror, but there are also staggered or diffracted wave trains like among which the component waves of the beam are distributed, and they teach us the undulatory nature of light and enable us to measure the wave length of its waves.

This process of ploughing a mirror-smooth surface of lustrous metal with parallel furrows, "ruling a grating" as it is called, should be ranked among the arts. Those who have practiced it with eminent success are fewer far than those who have attained to skill in any other art; and also it is that rarity, an art in which the primacy is conceded to Americans even by the Europeans—an uncontested primacy now nearly seventy years old, though of course America cannot claim the founder of this art. Fraunhofer met and wrestled with the difficulties which his transatlantic followers have almost overcome. In his time, as now, it was easy to rule tens of thousands of rough grooves roughly to the inch; the trouble lay, as still it lies, in making them identical and spacing them equally. Though the angles of deviation do not depend on the shape of the groove, it is important for the excellence of the grating that all the "lines" shall be alike, and even more important that their spacing shall not vary; while the more of them there are lying side by side, the sharper and more distinct are the paths of the diffracted wave trains.

Equality of spacing depends upon a screw, which is turned through a prearranged angle and is expected to advance through a definite distance carrying the future grating with it, whenever the diamond has completed one ruling and is waiting to begin the next. Screws as manufactured are not good enough, and anyone who aspires to be a maker of gratings must first of all procure the best available and then devote a long and tedious time to making it still better. Michelson used to say that the time required to perfect a screw varies as the cube of the number of lines which one wishes to rule by its aid; and so, the sharpness of the diffracted beams is bought at an enormous cost in patience and in perseverance. An institute of physical research is as proud of a notable grating by Rowland or Wood or Gale, as a picture gallery of an authentic Titian or Velasquez; and the promise of a new artistic talent is not more joyously welcomed than the rumor that someone is working to perfect a yet longer screw for making a grating still richer in lines.

As for alikeness of successive rulings, it depends on the endurance of the diamond. The ruling engine is sequestered in a room well protected from shock or chill, and after the temperature has settled down to constancy it is set in motion by some device manipulated from without and left to do its task in solitude. If before the process is over the diamond breaks, or suffers any important change in shape, the grating is good for nothing. This cannot be foreseen, one does not even know when it is likely to happen; to stop the ruling to see how things are going would be worse than digging up a seed to find how it is sprouting. The chance of such an accident being naturally greater the more numerous the lines, here is another obstacle to making gratings of unprecedented size.

Such labours would be excessive, if one were interested merely in amassing proof of the wave theory of light; their purpose is to improve the nicety with which we may distinguish the different wave lengths entering into the spectrum of any source of light, and the accuracy with which we may measure these wave lengths. These measurements, by the way, are among the most accurate in physics, which is to say, in science altogether; but there is no strong reason for stressing that precision here let me rather indicate roughly how large the customary wave lengths are. The values of wave length attached to the several trains: one sees that for convenient angles of diffraction, λ the wave length must be smaller but not very much smaller than d the spacing. Now, with gratings ruled with a few hundreds or thousands of lines to the centimetre, we do obtain convenient angles of diffraction for the various colored components of the visible spectrum; and, on making the measurements, it is found that the waves of visible light run about twenty thousand to the centimetre or fifty thousand to the inch.

The range of ë "in the visible" is roughly from .00004 of a centimetre for violet light to .00008 for red light. Light of the infrared has greater wave lengths, and when we start out to explore the infrared ocean we soon have to widen the spacing of our gratings, for a grating ceases to function at all when ë is greater than d. For radio waves we should require the lines to be inches, yards, nay even miles apart fortunately there are other ways of measuring their wave lengths, but this book is not concerned with them. Light of the ultraviolet has shorter waves than the visible, and as we sail farther and farther out over the ultraviolet ocean we find the angles of diffraction of an ordinary grating becoming smaller and smaller, so that eventually it becomes difficult and finally impossible to measure them at all. The spacing d cannot be diminished below such values as we have already given, for diamonds will engrave no finer grooves. The angles can be improved by projecting the beam of light very slantingly against the surface of the metal block, almost "at grazing incidence" as the term is; but even this device has its limits, though they are surprisingly far away it is possible to measure X-ray wave lengths ten thousand times shorter than those of visible light, for such is the scale of the X-rays. Near and beyond these limits, however, we may avail ourselves of gratings of inimitable fineness, constructed by Nature herself. These natural gratings are *crystals*.

"Crystal" is a word with misleading implications, and we suppose we should devote some space to brushing these away. The really important feature of a crystal, which is the ordering of the atoms in it, is a thing which no man ever sees, not even with the most powerful microscopes; and the things which are seen are often unimportant and not even confined to true crystals. For instance, we often use the word to denote the piece of glass over the face of a watch. This is a most unlucky habit, for if there is any solid substance in the world in which the real distinction of a crystal is feeble or missing, glass is certainly it. The earliest meaning of the Greek word *crystallos* was apparently ice, and this is not so bad, for ice is crystalline, though nothing in its outward aspect suggests that. "Crystal clarity" and "crystal purity" are just nonsensical phrases to a physicist, who knows that many an admirable crystal is opaque. There is, however, one idea associated with the word, which verges upon the essential.

Even in popular speech, "crystal" is likely to suggest a piece of matter which is not only glassy and transparent, but shaped into a strange and lovely form; a cube or column or a minaret, a pyramid or a pinnacle, with lustrous surfaces of exquisite smoothness divided from each other by ars of knife-edge sharpness. A perfectly formed crystal looks more like a creation of intelligent design than anything else in inorganic Nature; one would almost think it expressly contrived as a pleasure for the eye. It is a pleasure for the mind as well, for its surfaces and angles declare the inner truth. Glassiness and transparency have nothing whatever to do with this they are practically accidents; but the shape is a sign of that which is fundamental, the arrangement of the atoms. And yet, there may be a crystalline arrangement of the atoms, and no curiosity of outward form to suggest it. A perfectly rough and shapeless hunk of matter may be just as good a crystal as the loveliest diamond that ever was found. This we say to bring out the fact that, far from being infrequent, the crystalline state is almost universal among solids. Stones are mostly crystalline; a metal is a mass of tiny granular crystals, one or more of which may be increased to great size by techniques which are now well known; sand is pulverized crystal, brick is a mass of clay crystals baked together, and even wool and hair and cotton are crystalline to some degree.

Now, to state the essential feature of a crystal: it is a piece of matter in which the atoms are disposed in a superbly regular array in a neat geometrical pattern. The atoms of a crystal stand in ranks and files like soldiers on parade, instead of being huddled together in a disorderly crowd or sprinkled at random in an open space. Only, the parade is in three dimensions instead of two, and this makes analogies difficult to find. Regular arrays "lattices," they are called in two dimensions are rather familiar to everyone. The classic illustration is wallpaper, in which a design is repeated over and over again, both up and down and sideways; this is still usual in English books, but the trend of the art of interior decoration has made it less useful in America. The squares of a chessboard form a lattice, very limited in extent; the intersections of the streets in most American cities form lattices, though seldom perfect ones; the windows on the face of a very large skyscraper often make a magnificent two-dimensional lattice of vast expanse. But for examples of three-dimensional lattices, we have been able to think of only the intersections of the girders of a steel-frame building, as one sees them when the masonry coating is not yet on; and a friend has suggested the piles of cannon balls which are stacked up by ancient war memorials. But we want to make further use of our example of the windows; and therefore we introduce a picture of a notable architectural crystal, so to speak, arising on the waterfront of New York City.

Here the windows fall naturally into horizontal and vertical lines. Diagonal lines could, of course, be drawn across the lattice, which would cut through numerous windows; but the horizontal and the vertical lines are those on which the windows lie closest together, and it is they which dominate the arrangement. They are at right angles to each other, but the spacing is not quite the same along the two directions; such a lattice is called rectangular.

Now to come to the point: suppose that you were viewing this building from a very great distance, so that only its outline was distinguishable; or that you were approaching by sea on a misty day, so that the profile was clear but the windows not at all. Well, it is perfectly safe to say that, nevertheless, you would be sure that the close-packed lines of windows were parallel to the edges of the profile. You would be sure of this, even if you were in an airplane so rapidly tilting that you had lost the sense of the vertical. Never would you suspect that the lines of windows might be slanted at ten or twenty degrees to the edges of the building; you would accept the edges as guides to the lines of the windows, and you would be right. If, then, you were to approach close enough to distinguish the setbacks and the terraces, they would confirm the first impression; for their edges also are parallel to the principal edges, and to the dominant lines of windows.

This is how the crystallographer thinks when he observes a crystal. He sees, it may be, a substance which is a cube orb a heap of tiny cubes or an aggregate with the corners of cubes jutting out everywhere, such as rock salt or common salt or the mineral called galena. Often he sees terraces or setbacks, like the one which the isolated crystal in the figure shows. He infers that the dominant lines of atoms in the crystals make right angles with one another, like the dominant lines of windows on the face of the building. There have to be three families of such lines, instead of just the vertical and the horizontal families of lines which occur among the windows, so that the analogy is really with the crossings of the girders inside the building. Such a lattice is represented in Figure 7.4; of this kind are the lattices of rock salt, and of common salt, and of galena, and of many another substance. There are lattices of many other kinds, some of which manifest themselves in crystals of much greater beauty; but we should not pause to exhibit them, for in this place we are considering lattices not for themselves but for an ulterior end. I must, however, say something about the scale of these crystalline patterns.

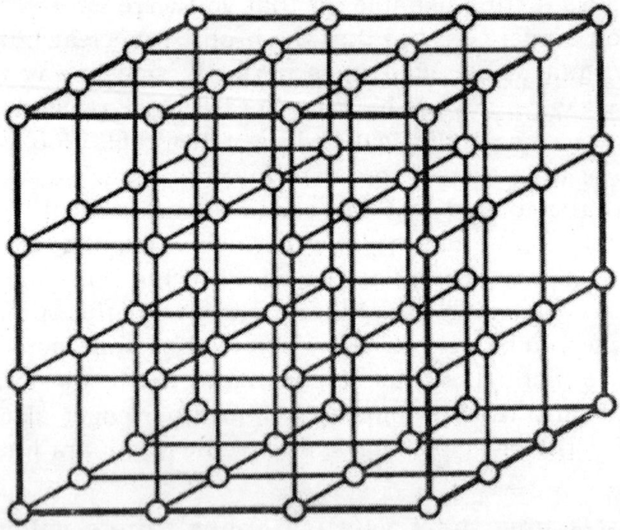

Figure 7.4. Lattice of a crystal of the cubic system.

No amount of looking upon a visible crystal, however intelligent and however well assisted by microscopes or measuring machines, will show how far apart the atoms of the lattice are; except, of course, that the failure proves them to be too small and too close together to be distinguished. The outward aspect of the crystal of rock salt teaches us that its particles are disposed like the dots in Figure 7.4 but gives us not the slightest indication as to whether the distance between adjacent atoms is a millionth, or a billionth, or a million-billionth of a centimetre. Thanks to these, we need only to measure the weight of a known volume, a cubic centimetre say, of the crystalline substance in which we are interested, and compare it with that of an atom: the ratio of the former to the latter is the number N of atoms in unit volume of the crystal, and the cube root of 1/N is the distance between adjacent atoms. One sees this by imagining the crystal subdivided into tiny cubes each one of which has eight adjacent atoms at its eight corners; call a the breadth of such a cube; a^3 is then the volume of each cubelet, and Na^3 is the total of their volumes, but this total is none other than one cubic centimeter. If the substance is a chemical compound, one must, of course, take an average of the weights of its several kinds of atoms; and there may be other intricacies, but none of them is insurmountable.

The general outcome is, that in a crystal *the atoms lie about a hundred million to the linear inch* a septillion to the cubic inch, another of those fantastic figures which spring from perfectly unquestionable reasoning, improbable as they seem! The number varies, of course, from one kind of crystal to another, but as a whole the variations are remarkably small. It seems as though atoms as a rule have a diameter not more, or in any case not much more, than a hundred millionth (10^{-10}) of an inch. The reason is that size unlike mass, unlike charge, unlike velocity is something which we cannot measure by any immediate method in the atomic world. No calipers can clamp such a particle in their jaws, no microscope can be focused upon it, no foot rule can be laid beside it. The directest evidence as to the breadth of atoms is that which we have just described; other estimates are made in various ways, and they agree rather well. Nuclei and electrons must be much smaller yet.

Atoms in a crystal thus are a thousand times or so more closely set together than the rulings of an artificial grating. If only we could engrave the lines of a grating at the rate of a hundred millions to the inch, how far out in the ultraviolet ocean we might sail! Wave trains of a wave length a thousand times smaller than those of visible light could then be deflected through the big convenient angles, which our gratings provide for us when visible light is in question; even wave lengths a hundred thousand times shorter would not be unmanageably small. No diamond can rule so finely spaced a sequence of troughs and ridges, as we said. But in 1911 it occurred to von Laue of Munich that a crystal itself is a grating one of the most fruitful ideas in all of modern physics, an idea of which the precious consequences are still far from being exhausted, perhaps never will be exhausted in our times.

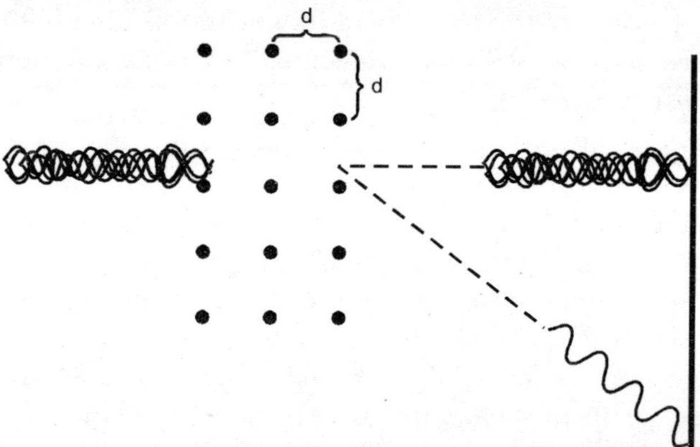

Figure 7.5. A mixture of wave trains of various wave lengths diffracted by the lattice of a crystal.

The dots of the earlier figure stood for the cross sections of long wires or grooves, to be imagined as stretching long distances forward and backward from the plane of the paper: wavelets springing from these wires or these grooves, at the instants when the wave crests reached them, spread out and fused themselves anew into diffracted wave crests. The dots of the later figure stand for individual atoms arranged in a crystalline lattice; and now one must imagine that this quadrilateral arrangement of atom dots is repeated over and over again, not only in the plane of the paper but forward and backward from that plane as though millions of copies of this page were stacked up, each carefully fitted in beside its two neighbours, and each separated from its two neighbors by just the distance *d* which separates any two adjacent atom dots upon the page.

If the reader will perform this feat of three-dimensional imagination, he will have a three-dimensional cubic lattice in mind. Falling upon this lattice from the left, we have tried to depict a beam composed of four wave trains of different wave lengths was falling upon the grating of wires or grooves. Departing from the lattice on the right,we have depicted one of the wave trains deflected or diffracted, just like the corresponding wave train departing from the artificial grating; but the other three we have depicted as going straight onward, which is what usually will happen.

This, indeed, is the distinctive feature of the three dimensional lattice. Every atom is an "irregularity" (to use the word I used before) from which a feeble wavelet springs when a wave crest sweeps across it: and for some few wave lengths those wavelets springing from all the myriad atoms will fuse together into staggered or diffracted waves, but for most wave lengths they will not. Most of the diffracted wave trains cannot appear because they shoot off obliquely at various angles to the plane of the paper. To return to my railroad simile: the crystal is a switchman who, when he sees a number of wave trains rushing toward him along a common track, switches a few of them aside each to a particular diverging track of its own, and sends the rest straight onward. If a beam of light comprising all wave lengths is sent across a grating of wires or grooves and strikes against a photographic plate beyond, the beam is broadened into a fan, and on the plate there appears a broad continuous blotch. But if the beam is sent across a crystal in place of the artificial grating, the fan is reduced to a spray of separate narrow rays each composed of a single wave train, and on the plate there appears a pattern of star-like spots where these several rays encounter it.

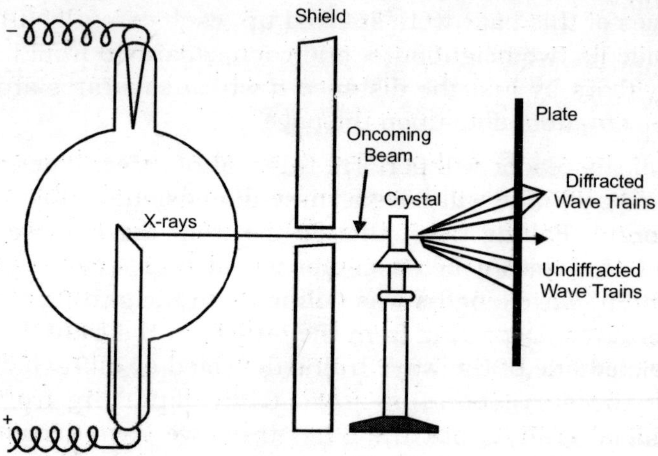

Figure 7.6. Arrangement for observing the diffraction-pattern ("Laue pattern") imposed by a single crystal upon a beam of X-rays composed of wave trains of a great diversity of wave lengths.

This is what Von Laue foretold; which represents a beam of X-rays emerging from a tube, passing through a channel which delimits it, and passing then through a crystal. Beyond the crystal, the beam is shown divided into several rays, which fall in separate places upon the plate beyond. There is nothing arbitrary nor casual about the directions of these rays. They are fixed by the crystalline structure that is to say, by the character of the lattice and by the spacing of the atoms of the lattice. They are disposed according to a beautiful and symmetrical geometry of their own; and upon the photographic plate which intercepts them there should appear a striking constellation, its stars not sprinkled at random but arranged in a formal pattern derivable and derived from the pattern of the atoms in the crystal.

Von Laue, as I said, foretold this for waves for waves sufficiently short, be it understood, because a crystal is like a grating of wires or scratches in that it is incapable of diffracting waves which are longer than its spacing. He did not affirm it with certainty for X-rays, since at that time it was not surely known that X-rays were undulatory. People were still inclined to draw a sharp antithesis between rays which are streams of corpuscles and rays which are trains of waves: few suspected even in part, and no one realized in full, that presently it was to be shown that a ray which is of either character must also be of the other. The question "are X-rays corpuscles or waves?" is now, a meaningless sequence of words; but in 1911 it seemed as indeed it still must seem, to anyone not specially prepared a real and vital question; and the weight of the evidence lay on the side of the corpuscles. It was, however, assured by a certain experiment which we will not pause to describe that if X-rays were wavelike their wave lengths must be about a thousand times smaller than those of visible light.

Having thought out the laws of the diffraction of waves by three-dimensional lattices, Von Laue had also the inspiration that crystals are just of the suitable spacing for diffracting the waves which X-rays must be, if X-rays are waves at all. Thus when he proposed the experiment to his colleagues Friedrich and Knipping at Munich, it was invested with the charm of the *experimentum crucis* the lure of the crucial experiment, the prospect of enthroning the one and destroying the other of two antagonistic theories, ever one of the strongest incentives to research. Friedrich and Knipping performed the experiment; they put the question to Nature, and the answer was returned to them in perhaps the most e*clatant* fashion in which question was ever answered: for the plate displayed the splendid constellation of sharp dots, due to diffracted wave trains and arranged in the exquisite order which Von Laue had foretold from the lattice of the crystal. Victory had come to the wave theory of the X-rays; but defeat had not come to its adversary, though this they did not know.

"Laue diffraction patterns"; not that first example which Friedrich and Knipping beheld, but a more luxuriant pattern obtained with a more complicated crystal. There are myriads of such pictures in the literature of physics and chemistry and mineralogy, and more are being taken every day, not because the waves require further proof, but for what is in a sense the opposite reason. The waves have ceased to be the object and become the agent of research; for every such pattern is testimony about the details of the crystal lattice which made it.

It was suggested above that we know the lattice-excepting for its scale, the spacing of its atoms from inspecting the shape of the crystal. So we do, in favourable cases; but many crystalline substances do not choose to assume the beautiful outward form which betrays the inward array. Metals, for example, usually conceal under rough and spotty exteriors a lattice which may be as nearly perfect as that of any diamond; and only a beam of short waves can reveal such a lattice, by letting itself be diffracted. Even in crystals excellently formed, of which the shape suggests the atomic array, there are many details of arrangement which only waves can disclose. The science of crystals has been enriched and broadened beyond all measure by this infusion of physics. So valuable to that science is the diffraction of waves that there is now a great variety of schemes for applying it and a vast diversity of apparatus and technique, most of which would probably never have been invented had the waves in themselves been the only object of our interest.

The beam of X-rays which falls upon the crystal is no longer a mixture of all wave lengths, but a "monochromatic" beam comprising one wave length only. Now the pattern on the plate will be pitifully shrunken. At worst, the constellation will be reduced to its big central spot, for the wave length may not be one of those which can be diffracted—the switchman of my simile may send the solitary wave train straight ahead. At best, i.e., if the wave train *is* diffracted, there will be just a few spots on the plate (not just one only, for if the waves can be diffracted at all their energy will be divided up among several rays shooting off in different directions through the crystal.) Now, suppose the crystal taken momentarily out of the beam and then replaced on its pedestal in a new orientation. The pattern of spots on the plate will no longer be the same. There may be just a few spots in new positions, or there may be none at all. Next, suppose this repeated over and over again until the crystal has been traversed by the beam in thousands or (better) millions of different directions, being newly oriented every time it is set upon the pedestal; and suppose that all this time the same plate receives the diffracted rays. At the end it will be found that all the spots on the plate are arranged in circular haloes or rings, and if the spots are numerous enough the rings will be uniform and smooth and very beautiful.

Actually the experiment would not be done in this way, which would take far too much trouble and time. The procedure is to place a great number of tiny crystals, oriented as nearly as possible at random, together in the path of the monochromatic beam. The spots from all of them (or rather, from all of those which are so oriented that they can diffract the wave trains) lie on rings on the plate, and if the little crystals are numerous enough the rings are uniform and smooth. One may get a mass of little crystals by crumbling or pulverizing a single big one wherefore the method, invented independently in 1915 by Debye and Scherrer of the Technical High School in Zurich and by Hull of the General Electric in Schenectady, is called the "powder method." Also, it may turn out that in a film or block of metal (or some other substance) the crystals are so small, so multitudinous, and so diversely oriented that magnificent rings are obtained simply by sending a wave train straight through the block or the film.

These haloes are glorious proof of the wave—and also they are the source of nearly all of our knowledge of the crystalline lattices of metals and many another substance. Would that we could present an adequate view of this knowledge, but if we were to attempt it, the programme of this book would soon be swamped. I must content myself with referring to a splendid example of these diffraction patterns, the frontispiece of the book. Yet the reader will gather from the caption that it is a pattern made not with X-rays, but with electrons. Wave and corpuscle now confront each other undissembled; their conflict and their compromise ask a chapter for themselves.

❑❑❑

8

Atomic Physics

Introduction

Atomic energy is the source of power for both nuclear reactors and nuclear weapons. This energy comes from the splitting (fission) or joining (fusion) of atoms. To understand the source of this energy, one must first understand the atom.

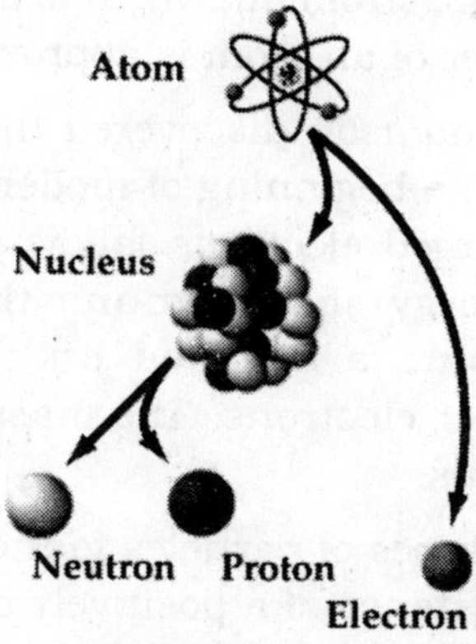

Figure 8.1. Components of the Atom

An atom is the smallest particle of an element that has the properties characterizing that element. Knowledge about the nature of the atom grew slowly until the early 1900s. One of the first breakthroughs was achieved by Sir Ernest Rutherford in 1911. He established that the mass of the atom is concentrated in its nucleus. He also proposed that the nucleus has a positive charge and is surrounded by negatively charged electrons, which had been discovered in 1897 by J.J. Thomson.

This theory of atomic structure was complemented by Niels Bohr in 1913. The Bohr atom placed the electrons in definite shells, or quantum levels. Understanding the atom continues to be a focus for many scientists.

Atomic Structure

An atom is a complex arrangement of negatively charged electrons arranged in defined shells about a positively charged nucleus. This nucleus contains most of the atom's mass and is composed of protons and neutrons (except for common hydrogen which has only one proton). All atoms are roughly the same size. A convenient unit of length for measuring atomic sizes is the angstrom (Å), which is defined as 1×10^{-10} meters. The diameter of an atom is approximately 2-3 Å.

In 1897, J.J. Thomson discovered the existence of the electron, marking the beginning of modern atomic physics. The negatively charged electrons follow a random pattern within defined energy shells around the nucleus. Most properties of atoms are based on the number and arrangement of their electrons. The mass of an electron is 9.1×10^{-31} kilograms.

One of the two types of particles found in the nucleus is the proton. The existence of a positively charged particle, a proton, in the nucleus was proved by Sir Ernest Rutherford in 1919. The proton's charge is equal but opposite to the negative charge of the electron. The number of protons in the nucleus of an atom determines what kind of chemical element it is. A proton has a mass of 1.67×10^{-27} kilograms.

The neutron is the other type of particle found in the nucleus. It was discovered by a British physicist, Sir James Chadwick. The neutron carries no electrical charge and has the same mass as the proton. With a lack of electrical charge, the neutron is not repelled by the cloud of electrons or by the nucleus, making it a useful tool for probing the structure of the atom.

Even the individual protons and neutrons have internal structure, called quarks. Six types of quarks exist. These subatomic particles cannot be freed and studied in isolation. Current research continues into the structure of the atom.

Atomic Isotopes

A major characteristic of an atom is its atomic number, which is defined as the number of protons. The chemical properties of an atom are determined by its atomic number and is denoted by the symbol Z. The total number of nucleons (protons and neutrons) in an atom is the atomic mass number. This value is denoted by the symbol A. The number of neutrons in an atom is denoted by N. Thus the mass of an atom is A = N + Z.

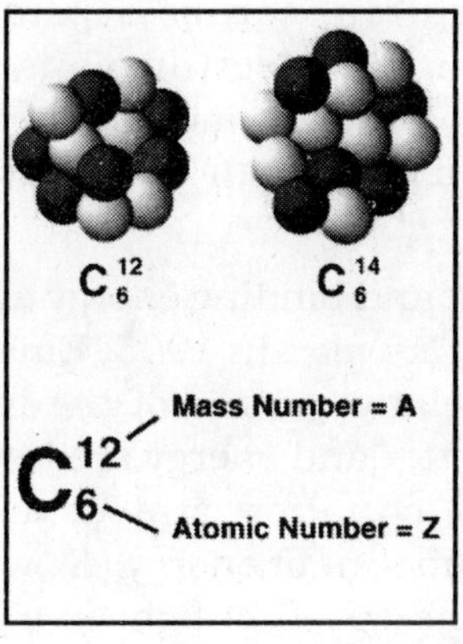

Figure 8.2. Nuclear Isotopes

Atoms with the same atomic number but with different atomic masses are called isotopes. Isotopes have identical chemical properties, yet have very different nuclear properties. For example, there are three isotopes of hydrogen. Two of these isotopes are stable, (not radioactive), but tritium (one proton and two neutrons) is unstable. Most elements have stable isotopes. Radioactive isotopes can also be created for many elements.

Einstein's Equation

The mass of the nucleus is about 1 percent smaller than the mass of its individual protons and neutrons. This difference is called the mass defect. The mass defect arises from the energy released when the nucleons (protons and neutrons) bind together to form the nucleus. This energy is called the binding energy. The binding energy determines which nuclei are stable and how much energy is released in a nuclear reaction. Very heavy nuclei and very light nuclei have low binding energies. This implies that a heavy nucleus will release energy when it splits apart (fission), and two light nuclei will release energy when they join (fusion).

The hydrogen 2 nucleus, for example, composed of one proton and one neutron, can be separated completely by supplying 2.23 million electron volts (MeV) of energy. Conversely, when a slowly moving neutron and proton combine to form a hydrogen 2 nucleus, 2.23 MeV are liberated.

The mass defect and binding energy are related by Albert Einstein's formula, $E = mc^2$. In 1905, Einstein developed the special theory of relativity. One of the implications of this theory was that matter and energy are interchangeable with one another. This equation states, a mass (m) can be converted into an amount of energy (E), where c is the speed of light. Because the speed of light is a large number and thus c squared is huge, a small amount of matter can be converted into a tremendous amount of energy. This equation is the key to the power of nuclear weapons and nuclear reactors.

Radioactive Decay

Radioactivity is the spontaneous disintegration of atomic nuclei. This phenomenon was first reported in 1896 by the French physicist Henri Becquerel. Marie Curie and her husband Pierre Curie contributed further to the understanding of radioactivity. Their research led to the discovery of two new radioactive elements, polonium and radium, and forced scientists to change their ideas about the structure of the atom.

Radioactivity is the result of an atom trying to reach a more stable nuclear configuration. The process of radioactive decay, can be achieved via three primary methods; a nucleus can change one of its neutrons into a proton with the simultaneous emission of an electron (beta decay), by emitting a helium nucleus (alpha decay), or by spontaneous fission (splitting) into two fragments. Often associated with these events is the release of high energy photons or gamma rays. There are some other method of radioactive decay, but they are more exotic in nature.

Each individual radioactive substance has a characteristic decay period or half-life. A half-life is the interval of time required for one-half of the atomic nuclei of a radioactive sample to decay. The radioactive isotope cobalt 60, which is used in radiation cancer therapy, has, for example, a half-life of 5.26 years. Thus after that interval, a sample originally containing 16 grams of cobalt 60 would contain only 8 grams of cobalt 60 and would emit only half as much radiation. After another interval of 5.26 years, the sample would contain only 4 grams of cobalt 60. Half-lives can range from thousands of years to milliseconds. Sometimes after undergoing radioactive decay, the new atom is still left in a radioactive form. This means that the atom will decay again as it attempts to reach a stable nuclear state.

Alpha Decay

In alpha decay, a positively charged particle, identical to the nucleus of helium 4, is emitted spontaneously. This particle, also known as an alpha particle, consists of two protons and two neutrons. It was discovered and named by Sir Ernest Rutherford in 1899.

α (alpha particle) = He_2^4

Plutonium 239 decays by alpha particle emission as follows:

$$Pu_{94}^{239} \xrightarrow[24,000\ \text{yrs}]{} U_{92}^{235} + He_2^4$$

(alpha particle)

Figure 8.3. Alpha Decay

Alpha decay usually occurs in heavy nuclei such as uranium or plutonium, and therefore is a major part of the radioactive fallout from a nuclear explosion. Since an alpha particle is relatively more massive than other forms of radioactive decay, it can be stopped by a sheet of paper and cannot penetrate human skin. A 4 MeV alpha particle can only travel about 1 inch through the air.

Although the range of an alpha particle is short, if an alpha decaying element is ingested, the alpha particle can do considerable damage to the surrounding tissue. This is why plutonium, with a long half-life, is extremely hazardous if ingested.

Beta Decay

Atoms emit beta particles through a process known as beta decay. Beta decay occurs when an atom has either too many protons or too many neutrons in its nucleus. Two types of beta decay can occur. One type (positive beta decay) releases a positively charged beta particle called a positron, and a neutrino; the other type (negative beta decay) releases a negatively charged beta particle called an electron, and an antineutrino. The neutrino and the antineutrino are high energy elementary particles with little or no mass and are released in order to conserve energy during the decay process. Negative beta decay is far more common than positive beta decay.

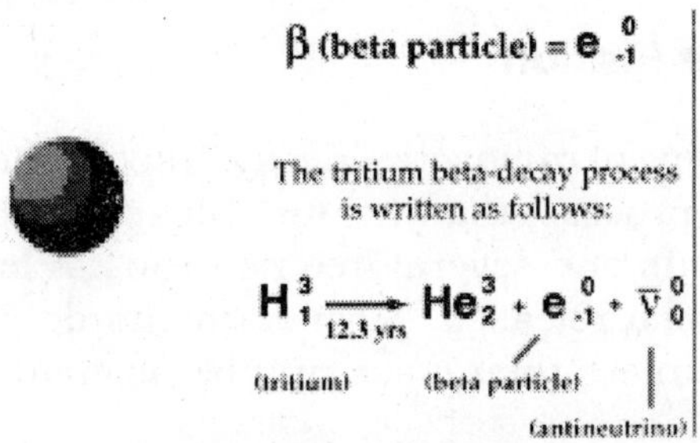

Figure 8.4. Beta Decay

This form of radioactive decay was discovered by Sir Ernest Rutherford in 1899, although the neutrino was not observed until the 1960s. Beta particles have all the characteristics of electrons. At the time of their emission, they travel at nearly the speed of light. A typical .5 MeV particle will travel about 10 feet through the air, and can be stopped by 1-2 inches of wood.

Gamma Rays

Gamma rays are a type of electromagnetic radiation that results from a redistribution of electric charge within a nucleus. Gamma rays are essentially very energetic X-rays; the distinction between the two is not based on their intrinsic nature but rather on their origins. X-rays are emitted during atomic processes involving energetic electrons. Gamma radiation is emitted by excited nuclei or other processes involving subatomic particles; it often accompanies alpha or beta radiation, as a nucleus emitting those particles may be left in an excited (higher-energy) state.

Gamma rays are more penetrating than either alpha or beta radiation, but less ionizing. Gamma rays from nuclear fallout would probably cause the largest number of casualties in the event of the use of nuclear weapons in a nuclear war. They produce damage similar to that caused by X-rays such as burns, cancer, and genetic mutations.

Spontaneous Fission

Another type of radioactive decay is spontaneous fission. In this decay process, the nucleus will split into two nearly equal fragments and several free neutrons. A large amount of energy is also released. Most elements do not decay in this manner unless their mass number is greater than 230.

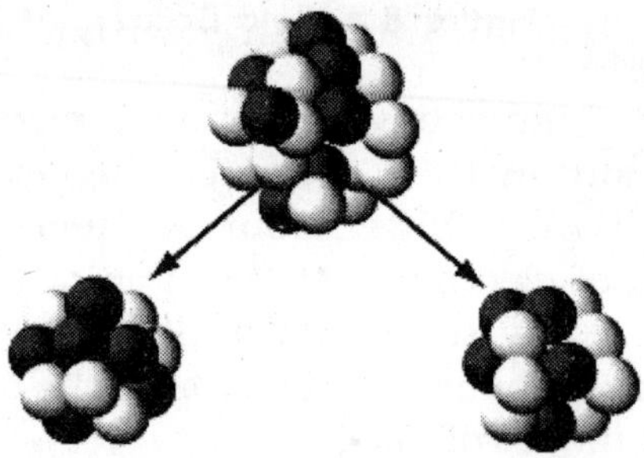

Figure 8.5. Spontaneous Fission

The stray neutrons released by a spontaneous fission can prematurely initiate a chain reaction. This means that the assembly time to reach a critical mass has to be less than the rate of spontaneous fission. Scientists have to consider the spontaneous fission rate of each material when designing nuclear weapons.

For example, the spontaneous fission rate of plutonium 239 is about 300 times larger than that of uranium 235. This forced scientists working on the Manhattan Project to abandon work on a gun-type design that used plutonium.

Atomic Theory

In chemistry and physics, atomic theory is a theory of the nature of matter, which states that matter is composed of discrete units called atoms, as opposed to the obsolete notion that matter could be divided into any arbitrarily small quantity. It began as a philosophical concept in ancient Greece and India and entered the scientific mainstream in the early 19th century when discoveries in the field of chemistry showed that matter did indeed behave as if it were made up of particles.

The word "atom" was applied to the basic particle that constituted a chemical element, because the chemists of the era believed that these were the fundamental particles of matter. However, around the turn of the 20th century, through various experiments with electromagnetism and radioactivity, physicists discovered that the so-called "indivisible atom" was actually a conglomerate of various subatomic particles (chiefly, electrons, protons and neutrons) which can exist separately from each other. In fact, in certain extreme environments such as neutron stars, extreme temperature and pressure prevents atoms from existing at all. Since atoms were found to be actually divisible, physicists later invented the term "elementary particles" to describe indivisible particles. The field of science which studies subatomic particles is particle physics, and it is in this field that physicists hope to discover the true fundamental nature of matter.

Modern Atomic Theory

Earliest Empirical Evidence: Near the end of the 18th century, two laws about chemical reactions emerged without referring to the notion of an atomic theory. The first was the law of conservation of mass, formulated by Antoine Lavoisier in 1789, which states that the total mass in a chemical reaction remains constant (that is, the reactants have the same mass as the products). The second was the law of definite proportions. First proven by the French chemist Joseph Louis Proust in 1799, this law states that if a compound is broken down into its constituent elements, then the masses of the constituents will always have the same proportions, regardless of the quantity or source of the original substance.

John Dalton studied and expanded upon this previous work and developed the law of multiple proportions: if two elements can together form more than one compound, then the ratios of the masses of the second element which combine with a fixed mass of the first element will be ratios of small integers. For instance, Proust had studied tin oxides and found that their masses were either 88.1% tin and 11.9% oxygen or 78.7% tin and 21.3% oxygen. Dalton noted from these percentages that 100 g of tin will combine either with 13.5 g or 27 g of oxygen; 13.5 and 27 form a ratio of 1:2. Dalton found an atomic theory of matter could elegantly explain this common pattern in chemistry — in the case of Proust's tin oxides, one tin atom will combine with either one or two oxygen atoms.

Dalton also believed atomic theory could explain why water absorbed different gases in different proportions: for example, he found that water absorbed carbon dioxide far better than it absorbed nitrogen. Dalton hypothesized this was due to the differences in mass and complexity of the gases' respective particles. Indeed, carbon dioxide molecules (CO_2) are heavier and larger than nitrogen molecules (N_2).

Dalton proposed that each chemical element is composed of atoms of a single, unique type, and though they cannot be altered or destroyed by chemical means, they can combine to form more complex structures (chemical compounds). This marked the first truly scientific theory of the atom, since Dalton reached his conclusions by experimentation and examination of the results in an empirical fashion.

In 1803 Dalton orally presented his first list of relative atomic weights for a number of substances. But he did not discuss there exactly how he obtained these figures. The method was first revealed in 1807 by his acquaintance Thomas Thomson, in the third edition of Thomson's textbook, *A System of Chemistry*. Finally, Dalton published a full account in his own textbook, *A New System of Chemical Philosophy*, 1808 and 1810.

Dalton estimated the atomic weights according to the mass ratios in which they combined, with hydrogen being the basic unit. However, Dalton did not conceive that with some elements atoms exist in molecules e.g. pure oxygen exists as O_2. He also mistakenly believed that the simplest compound between any two elements is always one atom of each (so he thought water was HO, not H_2O). This, in addition to the crudity of his equipment, resulted in his table being highly flawed. For instance, he believed oxygen atoms were 5.5 times heavier than hydrogen atoms, because in water he measured 5.5 grams of oxygen for every 1 gram of hydrogen and believed the formula for water was HO (an oxygen atom is actually 16 times heavier than a hydrogen atom).

The flaw in Dalton's theory was corrected in 1811 by Amedeo Avogadro. Avogadro had proposed that equal volumes of any two gases, at equal temperature and pressure, contain equal numbers of molecules (in other words, the mass of a gas's particles does not affect its volume). Avogadro's law allowed him to deduce the diatomic nature of numerous gases by studying the volumes at which they reacted. For instance: since two liters of hydrogen will react with just one litre of oxygen to produce two liters of water vapour (at constant pressure and temperature), it meant a single oxygen molecule splits in two in order to form two particles of water. Thus, Avogadro was able to offer more accurate estimates of the atomic mass of oxygen and various other elements, and firmly established the distinction between molecules and atoms.

In 1827, the British botanist Robert Brown observed that pollen particles floating in water constantly jiggled about for no apparent reason. In 1905, Albert Einstein theorized that this Brownian motion was caused by the water molecules continuously knocking the grains about, and developed a hypothetical mathematical model to describe it. This model was validated experimentally in 1908 by French physicist Jean Perrin, thus providing additional validation for particle theory (and by extension atomic theory).

Discovery of Subatomic Particles

Atoms were thought to be the smallest possible division of matter until 1897 when J.J. Thomson discovered the electron through his work on cathode rays. A Crookes tube is a sealed glass container in which two electrodes are separated by a vacuum. When a voltage is applied across the electrodes, cathode rays are generated, creating a glowing patch where they strike the glass at the opposite end of the tube. Through experimentation, Thomson discovered that the rays could be deflected by an electric field (in addition to magnetic fields, which was already known). He concluded that these rays, rather than being a form of light, were composed of very light negatively charged particles he called "corpuscles" (they would later be renamed electrons by other scientists).

Thomson believed that the corpuscles emerged from the molecules of gas around the cathode. He thus concluded that atoms were divisible, and that the corpuscles were their building blocks. To explain the overall neutral charge of the atom, he proposed that the corpuscles were distributed in a uniform sea of positive charge; this was the plum pudding model as the electrons were embedded in the positive charge like plums in a plum pudding (although in Thomson's model they were not stationary).

Discovery of the Nucleus

Thomson's plum pudding model was disproved in 1909 by one of his former students, Ernest Rutherford, who discovered that most of the mass and positive charge of an atom is concentrated in a very small fraction of its volume, which he assumed to be at the very centre.

In the gold foil experiment, Hans Geiger and Ernest Marsden (colleagues of Rutherford working at his behest) shot alpha particles at a thin sheet of gold, measuring their deflection with a fluorescent screen. Given the very small mass of the electrons, the high momentum of the alpha particles and the unconcentrated distribution of positive charge of the plum pudding model, the experimenters expected all the alpha particles to pass through the gold sheet without significant deflection. To their astonishment, a small fraction of the alpha particles experienced heavy deflection.

This led Rutherford to propose a planetary model in which a cloud of electrons surrounded a small, compact nucleus of positive charge. Only such a concentration of charge could produce the electric field strong enough to cause the heavy deflection.

First Steps Toward a Quantum Physical Model of the Atom

The planetary model of the atom had two significant shortcomings. The first is that, unlike planets orbiting a sun, electrons are charged particles. An accelerating electric charge is known to emit electromagnetic waves according to the Larmor formula in classical electromagnetism; an orbiting charge should steadily lose energy and spiral toward the nucleus, colliding with it in a small fraction of a second. The second problem was that the planetary model could not explain the highly peaked emission and absorption spectra of atoms that were observed.

Quantum theory revolutionized physics at the beginning of the 20th century, when Max Planck and Albert Einstein postulated that light energy is emitted or absorbed in discrete amounts known as quanta (singular, *quantum*). In 1913, Niels Bohr incorporated this idea into his Bohr model of the atom, in which an electron could only orbit the nucleus in particular circular orbits with fixed angular momentum and energy, its distance from the nucleus (i.e., their radii) being proportional to its energy. Under this model an electron could not spiral into the nucleus because it could not lose energy in a continuous manner; instead, it could only make instantaneous "quantum leaps" between the fixed energy levels. When this occurred, light was emitted or absorbed at a frequency proportional to the change in energy (hence the absorption and emission of light in discrete spectra).

Bohr's model was not perfect. It could only predict the spectral lines of hydrogen; it couldn't predict those of multielectron atoms. Worse still, as spectrographic technology improved, additional spectral lines in hydrogen were observed which Bohr's model couldn't explain. In 1916, Arnold Sommerfeld added elliptical orbits to the Bohr model to explain the extra emission lines, but this made the model very difficult to use, and it still couldn't explain more complex atoms.

Discovery of Isotopes

While experimenting with the products of radioactive decay, in 1913 radiochemist Frederick Soddy discovered that there appeared to be more than one element at each position on the periodic table. The term isotope was coined by Margaret Todd as a suitable name for these elements.

That same year, J.J. Thomson conducted an experiment in which he channeled a stream of neon ions through magnetic and electric fields, striking a photographic plate at the other end. He observed two glowing patches on the plate, which suggested two different deflection trajectories.

Thomson concluded this was because some of the neon ions had a different mass. The nature of this differing mass would later be explained by the discovery of neutrons in 1932.

Discovery of Nuclear Particles

In 1918, Rutherford bombarded nitrogen gas with alpha particles and observed hydrogen nuclei being emitted from the gas. Rutherford concluded that the hydrogen nuclei emerged from the nuclei of the nitrogen atoms themselves (in effect, he split the atom). He later found that the positive charge of any atom could always be equated to that of an integer number of hydrogen nuclei. This, coupled with the facts that hydrogen was the lightest element known and that the atomic mass of every other element was roughly equivalent to an integer number of hydrogen atoms, led him to conclude hydrogen nuclei were singular particles and a basic constituent of all atomic nuclei: the proton. Further experimentation by Rutherford found that the nuclear mass of most atoms exceeded that of the protons it possessed; he speculated that this surplus mass was composed of hitherto unknown neutrally charged particles, which were tentatively dubbed "neutrons".

In 1928, Walter Bothe observed that beryllium emitted a highly penetrating, electrically neutral radiation when bombarded with alpha particles. It was later discovered that this radiation could knock hydrogen atoms out of paraffin wax. Initially it was thought to be high-energy gamma radiation, since gamma radiation had a similar effect on electrons in metals, but James Chadwick found that the ionisation effect was too strong for it to be due to electromagnetic radiation. In 1932, he exposed various elements, such as hydrogen and nitrogen, to the mysterious "beryllium radiation", and by measuring the energies of the recoiling charged particles, he deduced that the radiation was actually composed of electrically neutral particles with a mass similar to that of a proton. For his discovery of the neutron, Chadwick received the Nobel Prize in 1935.

Quantum Physical Models of the Atom

In 1924, Louis de Broglie proposed that all moving particles particularly subatomic particles such as electrons exhibit a degree of wave-like behaviour. Erwin Schrodinger, fascinated by this idea, explored whether or not the movement of an electron in an atom could be better explained as a wave rather than as a particle. Schrödinger's equation, published in 1926, describes an electron as a wave function instead of as a point particle. This approach elegantly predicted many of the spectral phenomena that Bohr's model failed to explain. Although this concept was mathematically convenient, it was difficult to visualize, and faced opposition. One of its critics, Max Born, proposed instead that Schrödinger's wave function described not the electron but rather all its possible states, and thus could be used to calculate the probability of finding an electron at any given location around the nucleus. This reconciled the two opposing theories of particle versus wave electrons and the idea of wave-particle duality was introduced. This theory stated that the electron may exhibit the properties of both a wave and a particle. For example, it can be refracted like a wave, and has mass like a particle.

A consequence of describing electrons as waveforms is that it is mathematically impossible to simultaneously derive the position and momentum of an electron; this became known as the Heisenberg uncertainty principle after the theoretical physicist Walter Heisenberg, who first described it. This invalidated Bohr's model, with its neat, clearly defined circular orbits. The modern model of the atom describes the positions of electrons in an atom in terms of probabilities. An electron can potentially be found at any distance from the nucleus, but, depending on its energy level, tends to exist more frequently in certain regions around the nucleus than others; this pattern is referred to as its atomic orbital. The orbital come in a variety of shapes, manifesting from a simple sphere of the full helium orbital, to the dumbbell shape of the full neon orbital, with the nucleus in the middle.

❏❏❏

9

Semantic Institution of the Quantization Programme

Introduction

The dynamical variables of classical mechanics play two distinct roles. On the most primitive level, they are regarded as attributes of the physical system under investigation. Thus one frequently employs the symbols q and p to denote the position and momentum respectively, of a particular degree of freedom of a physical system. In this sense the dynamical variables q and p are attributes of the physical system contributing to the specifications of its instantaneous state, their evolution in time being determined by the dynamics of the physical system. The dynamical laws of classical physics, however, are found to have a striking symmetry which enables one to map physically distinct system into each other provided they have the same number of degrees of freedom. This symmetry can be characterized by an abstract group, the canonical group, namely the group of transformations which leaves invariant the symplectic form when treated as a tensor field over an even-dimensional manifold dubbed the "classical phase space". The elements of this canonical group in the infinitesimal neighborhood of the identity can be realized by arbitrary functions of the dynamical variables. The commutators of the infinitesimal elements is then realized by the Poisson brackets of the corresponding functions. In this sense the dynamical variables play a more formal role. They may be regarded as operators which generate infinitesimal mappings of classical systems upon each other. While the operator properties of the dynamical variables are more remote from our primitive physical intuition, they play a vital role in enabling us to identify at least some of the abstract symbols occurring in a given physical theory with measurements performed in nature. It should be evident that once we have permitted the possibility of different physical theories to be mapped upon each other, the identification of symbols with measurements becomes a non-trivial matter.

In quantum theory, the distinction between the operator and the attribute aspect of the dynamical variables is more transparent. The symmetry of the dynamical laws in quantum theory is that of the unitary mappings in the Hilbert space. The dynamical variables are most directly identified as operators which generate the infinitesimal unitary mappings. The commutators of the infinitesimal unitary mappings are now realized by the algebraic commutators of the abstract symbols which represent the dynamical variables. The correspondence principle, which enables us to relate at least some of the dynamical variables of a classical theory with those of the related quantum theory, employs in a vital way the intimate relationship between the operator properties of the dynamical variables and the means by which they are measured in nature. Measurements, of course, are neither "classical" nor "quantum", for those words refer only to theories by means of which we hope to understand the significance of the actual operations occurring in performing the measurements.

Unlike the corresponding situation in classical theories, attributes of quantum systems cannot be realized by the same symbols which realize the operators. Rather, the attributes, that is the numerical consequences resulting from the performance of measurements, are now realized by the eigen values of the associated operators.

In order to initiate the procedure of canonical quantization one selects a set of fundamental classical dynamical variables q_i, p_j whose Poisson brackets are

$$[q_i, q_j] = [p_i, p_j] = 0 \qquad \ldots(9.1)$$

These relations are preserved under arbitrary canonical transformations, thus the formal identification of these variables is by no means unique. One then associates with each variable q_i, p_j a corresponding Hermitian operator Q_i, P_j such that their algebraic commutators satisfy

$$[q_i, p_j] = \delta_{ij}. \qquad \ldots(9.2)$$

(We are assuming units such that h = 1. The factor i occurs due to our employment of Hermitian operators rather than infinitesimal unitary ones.)

Von Neumann's theorem asserts that the set of operators which satisfy Eqn. (9.2) is unique up to a unitary transformation. In view of the fact that the classical variables which satisfy Eqn. (9.1) are unique up to a canonical transformation, it is clear that the initial selection of a canonically transformed set of classical dynamical variables would merely result in a unitarily transformed set of corresponding quantum dynamical variables. It would therefore appear that the canonical quantization of a given classical theory is insensitive to the particular choice of initial fundamental variables employed.

However, more is demanded in the procedure of quantization than the mere correspondence of basic dynamical variables. A physical system is frequently characterized by the dynamics which it satisfies. By "dynamics" we mean that there exists a well-defined relationship between the motion of a system in space and its evolution in time. Thus the dynamics of a physical system is determined by a constraining relationship between the operator which generates the mapping of the system in time, usually called the Hamiltonian, and the operators which generate the mappings of the system in space. More specifically, the dynamics of a physical system is generally characterized by a functional relationship

$$h = h(q_i, p_j) \qquad (9.3)$$

where h is the Hamiltonian of the system. Thus if $h = p2/2m$ we call such a system a free particle of mass m, while if $h = (p2/2m) + 1/2\, kq^2$ we call such a system a simple harmonic oscillator of mass m and spring constant k. It is important to note at this point that such a characterization of physical systems is not invariant under canonical transformations.

A critical step in the construction of a quantum theory is the requirement that the operator generating the evolution of the quantum system in time, also called the Hamiltonian, satisfies a constraint of the same functional form (as nearly as possible consistent with it being a Hermitian operator) as function of the fundamental quantum dynamical variables, as its corresponding classical counterpart. Thus

$$H = H(Q_i, P_j) = h(Q_i, P_j) \qquad ...(9.4)$$

where by the second equality we mean the same functional form as occurs in the corresponding classical expression, Equation (9.3) . Thus, the Hamiltonian for a quantum free particle of mass m is $H = P2/2m$, while the quantum simple harmonic oscillator Hamiltonian is $H = (P/2m) + 1/2\, k\, Q^2$.

If the correspondence of dynamics as realized by Eqn. (9.4) , were preserved under the action of the canonical transformations of the classical variables q_i, p_j and the corresponding unitary image of these transformations acting on the quantum variables Q_i, P_j, we could assert that the procedure of canonical quantization is invariant under canonical transformations. However this is not the case. The difficulty stems from the fact that under canonical transformations the classical Hamiltonian transforms as a scalar field over the phase space spanned by the dynamical variables q_i, p_j, whereas under unitary transformations the quantum Hamiltonian transforms as an operator, that is, as a Hermitian tensor, in the Hilbert space. Thus, although the transformation law for the q_i, p_j can be coordinated with those of the Q_i, P_j, the coordination cannot be preserved for h and H. In fact, while the functional form of H is preserved under unitary transformations, the functional form of h will in general change under canonical transformations.

We shall demonstrate this critical point by considering an infinitesimal canonical transformation which is simply an extended point transformation. Let us take for our example the infinitesimal generator

$$c = \text{UI+03B5}\ p\, q^2. \qquad \ldots(9.5)$$

Thus, the infinitesimal mapping generated by c is

$$q + {}^{-} - q = \delta\, q = [q, c] = \varepsilon\, q^2 \qquad \ldots(9.6)$$

$$p + {}^{-} - p = \delta\, p = [p, c] = 2\, \varepsilon\, pq.$$

Suppose that the classical system which we are considering has the Hamiltonian

$$h = \frac{p^2}{2m} + V(q) \qquad \ldots(9.7)$$

We are interested in the change in the functional form of the Hamiltonian as a function of the dynamical variables due to the transformation generated by c. In view of the fact that the Hamiltonian is regarded as a scalar under canonical transformations, we find

$$h\,(q, p) = h + {}^{-}\,(q + {}^{-}, p + {}^{-}) = h + {}^{-}\,(q + \delta\, q, p + \delta\, p). \qquad \ldots(9.8)$$

We therefore find for the change in the functional form of the Hamiltonian, to the first order in ε,

$$\bar{\delta}h \equiv \bar{h}(q,p) - h(q,p)$$
$$= -\varepsilon\left(\frac{\partial h}{\partial q}\delta q + \frac{\partial h}{\partial p}\delta p\right)$$
$$= -[a,c] \qquad \text{...(9.9)}$$

For the particular choice of c, Eq. (9.5), we have

$$\bar{\delta}h = \varepsilon\left(\frac{2p^2q}{m} - V'(q)q^2\right). \qquad \text{...(9.10)}$$

The functional form of the Hamiltonian has evidently been altered in a substantial way. This property of canonical transformations, of altering the functional form of the Hamiltonian is, of course, one of its principal and well-known virtues.

The Hermitian operator which we can associate with the classical generator of Eqn. (9.5) is

$$C = \varepsilon\, 1/2\, (PQ^2 + Q^2 P). \qquad \text{...(9.11)}$$

The infinitesimal mapping generated by C is, via Eqn. (9.2)

$$Q + {}^{-} - Q = \delta\, Q = -\, i\, [Q, C] = \varepsilon\, Q^2\, P + {}^{-}$$
$$-\, P = \delta\, P = -\, i\, [P, C] = -\, \varepsilon\, (QP + PQ). \qquad \text{...(9.12)}$$

Unlike the analogous situation in classical theory, the Hamiltonian of quantum theory transforms as a Hermitian tensor, that is, it transforms via the same law as do the operators Q and P. Thus

$$\bar{H} - H \equiv \delta H = -i[H,C]$$
$$= -\varepsilon\left(\frac{P^2Q + 2PQP + QP^2}{2m} - V'(Q)Q^2\right) \qquad \text{...(9.13)}$$

or, to first order in ε

$$\bar{H} = \frac{P^2}{2m} + V(Q) - \varepsilon\left(\frac{P^2Q + 2PQP + QP^2}{2m} - V'(Q)Q^2\right) \quad \ldots(9.14)$$

This expression corresponds to the classical change in value of the Hamiltonian, rather than the change in functional form. To obtain the change in functional form we must reexpress $H + ^{-}$ in terms of the transformed operators $Q + ^{-}$ and $P + ^{-}$. Thus from Eq. (9.12) , to order ε we have

$$Q = Q + ^{-} - \varepsilon\, Q + ^{-}2 \quad \ldots(9.15)$$

$$P = P + ^{-} + \varepsilon(Q + ^{-}P + ^{-} + \varepsilon\, Q + ^{-})$$

and consequently

$$P^2 = [P+^{-} + \varepsilon\,(Q+^{-}\,P+^{-} + P+^{-}\,Q+^{-}] \cdot$$

$$[P + ^{-} + \varepsilon\,(Q + ^{-}\,P + ^{-} + P + ^{-}\,Q + ^{-}] \quad \ldots(9.16)$$

$$= P+^{-}2 + \varepsilon\,(P+^{-}2\,Q+^{-} + 2\,P+^{-}\,Q+^{-}\,P+^{-} + Q+^{-}\,P+^{-}2).$$

Substituting Eqns. (9.15) and (9.16) into Eqn. (9.14) we find to first order in ε

$$\bar{H} = \frac{P^2}{2m} + V(\bar{Q}) \quad \ldots(9.17)$$

Therefore, as we have already anticipated, there is no change in the functional form of the quantum Hamiltonian! It is this discrepancy in the behavior of the classical and quantum Hamiltonians under corresponding transformations, which gives rise to the need for assigning preferred status to some particular set of classical dynamical variables when seeking to construct the corresponding quantum theory. Only under very special transformations do the processes of canonical transformation and canonical quantization commute.

Semantics of Dynamical Variables

It is of interest to inquire into the method of selection of the preferred dynamical variables referred to in the previous section. The clue to their selection is the well-known dictum that one must quantize only in "rectangular coordinates". Of course, it is not a satisfactory state of affairs to have so basic a criterion stated in a coordinate-dependent manner. In fact, it becomes particularly illuminating to determine the invariant criterion for the selection of the preferred canonical variables.

The space-time which is the arena of physics has a preferred isometry group, the Galilean group for non-relativistic physics or the Poincare group for special relativistic physics. The given isometry group singles out a preferred set of vector fields on the space which are a solution of an invariant differential equation known as Killing's equation. By selecting four commuting Killing directions we obtain a preferred set of space-time coordinates determined up to the transformations available in the isometry group. The three spatial coordinates so obtained induce a preferred coordinatization of the classical configuration space, and the preferred time-like coordinate yields a corresponding coordinatization of the tangent bundle over the configuration space. Finally, if we are given a dynamics, say in the form of a Lagrangian $L(q_i$, q + ·*i*), we can construct the momentum pi canonically conjugate to the chosen set of qi via the usual relation

$$p_i \equiv \frac{\partial L}{\partial q_i} \qquad \text{...(9.18)}$$

thereby obtaining a preferred coordinatization of the cotangent bundle, that is, the classical phase space. The essential point of this construction is that for the purposes of quantization a vital role is played by the assumed isometries of the space-time.

Examining the classical dynamical variables so obtained, that is, the q_i and p_j, we discover that upon viewing them in their operator aspect they generate the canonical mappings associated with the space-time isometries. In fact, upon closer inspection, we discover that it precisely this association of the preferred dynamical variables with the space-time isometrics which plays a critical role in enabling us to relate their values to the output of given measuring devices. Until such a relationship is established between the abstract symbols of the theory and measuring devices, our symbols are purely formal, satisfying well-defined syntactic laws of manipulation, but having no semantic content. Thus, the semantic content of a physical theory fundamentally is attained only upon establishing a relationship between the operator aspect of a given symbol and an isometry of space-time.

It now becomes clear why the program of canonical quantization places such critical emphasis on the association of certain classical commutators with corresponding quantum commutators. Not all classical commutation relations are preserved in the transition to quantum theory. An inspection of those commutation relations which are preserved intact in this transition reveals that it is precisely those commutation relations associated with the space-time isometry group! From our present perspective we therefore see that it is precisely the semantic content of the fundamental dynamical variables which is preserved by the procedure of canonical quantization. This is as it should be, for the relationship between the abstract symbols and the measurements which give them semantic content must be assumed ab initio, that is, before we set about to discover the correct (syntactic) laws which these symbols must satisfy.

Having thus identified the deeper significance of the program of canonical quantization let us complete the description of the procedure. The sub-group of the canonical group whose Lie algebra is preserved under quantization is the sub-group of linear transformations of the preferred phase space coordinates constructed above. (It is isomorphic to the symplectic group and contains as a sub-group the space-time isometries.) The quantization is completed by requiring that this symplectic group be represented by unitary mappings of a Hilbert space in such a fashion that the specific algebraic form of the mapping between the tangent bundle over the configuration space and the cotangent bundle, when expressed as a function of the preferred phase space coordinates, be preserved.

General Relativity

In an effort to construct a quantum theory of gravitation it would appear necessary first to expose the semantic content of the basic dynamical variables occurring in the general theory of relativity. In that theory, the preferred space-time group is no longer the Galilean or Poincaré group, but rather the Einstein group, that is, the group of four dimensional curvilinear coordinate transformations. It would therefore appear at first sight that the Einstein group should play a preferred role in the construction of a quantum theory of gravitation. However the Einstein group is generated by the constraints of the theory and must be eliminated in order to obtain the gauge-invariant observables of the theory appropriate for quantization. Having thereby lost the preferred status of the space-time group, one could investigate the possibility of preserving some arbitrarily chosen sub-algebra of the classical observables as a set of linear mappings of the vector space. However, such a procedure is hardly unique, and is devoid of any semantic content. It is not clear what relation it would bear to quantization as we previously understood the procedure. Rather than abandon all hope of a unique quantization of gravitation with a corresponding semantic identification of the observables, we can reimpose a preferred space-time group by the device of requiring restrictive boundary conditions on the class of solutions which we shall permit.

❐❐❐

10

Significance of Philosophy to Physics

Introduction

An Elementary Analysis of Physics

Physics may be viewed variously as:

P_1 : a body of knowledge;

P_2 : a discipline of study;

P_3 : a social institution.

These ways of viewing physics are not independent since the body of knowledge provides the raw material (background assumptions, problems, etc.) for the individuals following the discipline and grows according to their success, while the individuals in their corporate pursuit of knowledge make up the social institution. Nonetheless, P_1, P_2 and P_3 are distinguishable. Furthermore, they should be distinguished in any discussion of the relevance of philosophy to physics so that it is clearer what is being affirmed or denied, and so that one may assess the importance of a thesis more readily, for it is obviously a weightier matter to assert philosophy is relevant to P_1 (in symbols , letting '*M*' — for metaphysics — stand for philosophy, since 'P' is already in use)

$$M \xrightarrow{r} P_1$$

than it is to assert philosophy is relevant to P_3, since

$$M \xrightarrow{r} P_1$$

implies

$$M \xrightarrow{r} P_3 ,$$

but not *vice versa*. (In some cases,

$$M \xrightarrow{r} P_2$$

implies

$$M \xrightarrow{r} P_1 ,$$

for example if philosophical considerations were to clarify problems of method which in turn led to changes in P_1 ; but in other cases, not, for example if philosophical considerations were relevant merely to the state of mind of the research worker, giving him a greater understanding of what he was doing or enhancing his incentive to subject himself to the discipline. Even so, he might work more successfully as a result and thus affect P_1.)

I aim to show not only that

$$M \xrightarrow{r} P_1 ,$$

but also, and even independently,

$$M \xrightarrow{r} P_2 ,$$

and

$$M \xrightarrow{r} P_3 .$$

It is by no means my concern to show that all philosophy is relevant to physics on the contrary, we think a great deal of philosophical discussion is quite irrelevant but only to show that some philosophy is relevant to physics in all its aspects.

Since 'relevance' names a key concept in my thesis, it behaves me to give at least a cursory account of the meaning of the term. The notion of relevance is tricky since it involves the notion of propensity — which has not yet been satisfactorily elucidated in the literature and the notion of making a difference, which is a sort of causal concept. Operationally, we could say *X* is relevant to *Y* if and only if a change in *X* (ΔX) over an interval of time Δt implies a change in $Y(\Delta Y)$ over some corresponding interval Δt?:

$$X \xrightarrow{r} Y =_{df} (\Delta X \neq 0)_{\Delta t} \rightarrow (\Delta Y \neq 0)_{\Delta t'} .$$

Superficially this definition is satisfactory since we should certainly want to say that if changes in *X* lead to changes in *Y*, *X* is relevant to *Y*. But *X* may be relevant to *Y* even if some changes in *X* do not result in changes in *Y* and even if neither *X* nor *Y* changes. In this latter case we might want to say that a change in *X* might cause a change in *Y*. Thus we should prefer to say, *X* is relevant to *Y* if and only if changes in *X* have a propensity to lead to changes in *Y*. (Prop for propensity):

$$X \xrightarrow{r} Y =_{df} \text{Prop}\left[(\Delta X \neq 0)_{\Delta t} \rightarrow (\Delta Y \neq 0)_{\Delta t'}\right] \neq 0 .$$

Perhaps this is as deep an analysis as is needed for the purposes of this chapter.

An Elementary Analysis of Philosophy

We propose to view philosophy, primilarly, as a discipline of study, and to analyse it according to the problems under study. Consequently, we shall also have in view the aspect of philosophy as a body of knowledge, namely, as a variety of answers to philosophical problems. It is not my intention to argue either way on the question of the relevance to physics of philosophy as a social institution. We wish to engage my readers' attention, specifically, in inquiry into the problem of the relevance to physics of the study of some philosophical problems. Philosophical problems cluster in five main groups round central questions:

1. What is there, basically?
2. How do we know what there is?
3. How do we learn what there is to know?
4. How is what we know rationally ordered?
5. What values (and dysvalues) are conserved or created by our pursuit of knowledge?

Corresponding to five divisions of philosophy:

M_1 : Ontology (Greek *ontos*: being).

M_2 : Epistemology (Greek *episteme*: knowledge).

M_3 : Methodology (Greek *methodos*: mode of inquiry).

M_4 : Logic.

M_5 : Axiology (Greek *axios*: valuable) (including ethics and aesthetics).

Let us consider these divisions briefly, in turn.

Ontology

Consider physics as a body of knowledge (P_1). Baldly, physics is then a set of sentences, some specific, some general, some in ordinary languages, some in technical symbols, containing terms which name entities or properties of entities, and express relations between them. In a grossly oversimplified fashion, we might represent physics as a set of sentences of type (i):

(i) $F a$

where 'a' names an object and 'F' a property; and a set of sentences of type (ii):

(ii) $(x)_A (F x)$

where 'x' is a variable naming members of a class A. The entities and properties named may be deemed observable or unobservable. Empirical laws in physics usually generalize observable properties of observable entities, while theories proper may include unobservable (perhaps fictitious) properties of observable entities and even unobservable (perhaps fictitious) entities.

Consider physics as a discipline (P_2). It is usually understood (perhaps incorrectly) that an aim of physics is to say what sort of things the universe is made of and what the properties of these things are. This is one form of the central ontological question. As disciplines, ontology and physics share direction and aim. Hence, we should be able to view P_1 as a subclass of ontology, viewed as a body of knowledge. This should not be a surprising result, since, historically, some ontological theories have been early forms of physical theories. Some ontology not yet physics may be physics of the future. From this point of view, ontology is certainly relevant to physics. In addition we might view ontological theories as frameworks for the development of physical theories and for their interpretation. All this has been very nicely discussed by Agassi.

An example of an unresolved ontological dispute which is not without significance in physics is the problem of the deterministic character of the universe. For example, it is generally agreed that probabilities are involved in quantum theory but it remains unsolved what is being said about the world when this is agreed. Is the world at least partially indeterministic, in fact? That is, is chance objective? Or is it simply the case that we have not yet found the deterministic laws underlying quantum theory? Or should we understand the probabilities as always associated with our ignorance?. In addition to its interpretative significance any metaphysical (ontological) framework used to interpret physical theory will be significant in directing the course of future research since it will pose problems worth trying to solve which will be different from the problems posed by rival ontologies. Hence

$$M_1 \xrightarrow{r} P_1$$

and

$$M_1 \xrightarrow{r} P_2 .$$

A second domain of relevance is the debate over what physical theories are about. Two questions are usually confused here: the question whether terms in physical theories are intended to refer genuinely to the physical world or are merely ficittious, and the question whether the real world or only the world of appearances is accessible to scientific inquiry. The history of the confusion is interesting but we shall not retell it here. More recently the confusion has been compounded by the distinction between observables and unobservables. Let T be the class of terms occurring in theories in physics; let G be the sub-class of terms thought to refer genuinely; F the sub-class thought to be fictitious; let R be the sub-class referring to the real world; A to the apparent world; let O be the sub-class of terms naming observables; U, unobservables; such that:

$$G \cap F = \emptyset; R \cap A = \emptyset; 0 \cap U = \emptyset,$$

then

$$T = G \cup F; T = R \cup A; T = 0 \cup U.$$

Theories about the manner in which the sub-class boundaries are related to each other are many and varied. One of the earliest is naive realism, which may perhaps be presented as:

$$U = F = A = \emptyset, \text{ hence } T = O = G = R. \quad (1)$$

Naive realism, the theory that the world really is just what it appears to be on careful inspection by a sober, alert, intelligent (etc.) observer, is a very plausible theory. It was not significantly undermined by such arguments as those presented by Descartes as to why we should doubt the veracity of perceptions. Nonetheless a major problem for philosophers of the seventeenth and eighteenth centuries was to account for empirical knowledge. Furthermore this problem was never solved. Here it suffices to note that the problem what physical theories might properly be said to be about was made more difficult by a justificationary constraint. Thus, if $(x)_A\ (Px)$ represents a law in physics, then, it was thought A could refer genuinely to the real world only if the members of A were knowable, in the sense that it may be known that they exist, and hence, what some of their properties are. (If the members of A are not knowable, then the reference is fictitious.) But members of A were thought to be knowable only if their existence (and hence some of their properties) could be proved or, in some strong sense, justified. KANT thought that this latter requirement could not be met for the real world (that is, for any thing-in-itself), hence he dropped the idea that

$G \cap R \neq \emptyset$.

A further distinction was that between concepts which were supposed to be derived from experience and those which were invented (conjectured). Let C be the class of conjectured terms in physical theories and I the class of terms inferred from experience (by induction) so that $T = C \cup I$ and $C \cap I = \emptyset$. Further let J be the class of terms we are (whether inductively or not) justified in using, while S is the class of purely speculative terms or of terms used in a purely speculative fashion, such that $T = J \cup S$ and $J \cap S = \emptyset$. Then we may distinguish DESCARTES'S intellectualist view, (2),

from BACON'S inductivist view, (3):

$S = \emptyset;\ I = \emptyset;\ C = J = G = R,$ (2)

$S = \emptyset;\ C = \emptyset;\ I = J = G = R.$ (3)

Kant's theory to which we have already referred is perhaps:

$R = \emptyset;\ C \cup I = J = G = A.$ (4)

Positivists reacted against Kant's pessimism about knowledge of the real world without dropping the justificationary constraint. They identified what could not be known with what could not be observed. Their view may be represented thus:

$O = J = G = R; U = S = F \neq \varnothing$. (5)

With their view that justified physical theories might contain fictitious and unjustified terms they introduced an interesting note of corrigibility into the theory of physical theories; and, in addition, reintroduced instrumentalism, the theory that physical theories are *merely* instruments for prediction, hence it is a matter of indifference what terms are used as long as the phenomena are saved.

Popper rejected instrumentalism, but went further than the positivists in loosening the justificationary constraint. Popper suggested that it be dropped altogether: all knowledge was to be thought corrigible. Under Popper's view, unobservable terms may be genuine and observable terms may be unjustified. Hence Popper allowed for a more sophisticated version of realism. His view appears to be:

$A = \varnothing; I = \varnothing; J = \varnothing;$ hence $T = R = C = S; G \cap U \neq \varnothing$. ...(6)

This is the theory we endorse (conjecturo-critical realism). The question of occult qualities will be taken up again later.

The major realist component of $A = \varnothing$, may be thought to imply that no phenomenal terms enter physical theory. Terms referring to actual objects or to their apparent properties (colour, texture, etc.) do occur in physics, of course, but they occur in reports of observations or in instructions in experimental physics, rather than in physical theory proper. Hence, P_1 contains sentences in which phenomenal terms occur, while T does not. Whenever a theory is to be tested, part of the work to be done in preparing it for the test is to supplement the theory with assumptions enabling statements about observations to be deduced. In reply to Kant, we may perhaps urge that theoretical physics, which represents symbolically a possible physical world, is intended to represent more or less closely the real world and thus to serve as an explanation of appearances which differ from the postulated real world considerably. Furthermore, although we cannot prove that the entities we posit exist (or have the properties we ascribe to them), our supposition that they do enables us to explain appearances in a non-arbitrary fashion, and is corrigible under criticism, including empirical criticism. We contend that different views on the question what physical theories are about introduce into P_1 different interpretations of the symbols used in theoretical physics and hence, again,

$$M_1 \xrightarrow{r} P_1.$$

Furthermore, these different views affect the account we give of the discipline. Hence

$$M_1 \xrightarrow{r} P_2$$

Epistemology

In the Western intellectual tradition it has customarily been supposed that a sufficiently large number of fundamental truths are either self evident, or may readily be proved. Any rational man (obviously the best kind to be) would hold all and only those views which were self-evident or demonstrable. By contrast, on the one hand, the dogmatist was thought to be the man who held tenaciously to what could not be proved (or even to what could be disproved) while, on the other hand, the skeptic was thought to be the man who stubbornly refused to accept what "rational" men thought obvious or demonstrable. In what follows, we depart from the Western tradition and advert to skepticism, of a rather special kind. The epistemological problem raised by the challenge offered by early men of science (Copernicus, Galileo, Descartes, Boyle, Newton, etc.) to establish learning was 'How do we know what there is to know?' As might have been expected, given the rational tradition, this question was, more specifically: 'What warrant can we give, what justification, for what we claim to know?' Alternatively 'What authority may we cite . . .?' Two authorities vied for the role: the intellect and experience. It did not take long in the modern period for it to be clear that the intellect would not do as authority in science. On the other hand, scientists and philosophers still have not quite given up hope for experience as the authority to follow. Moreover, the theory that experience is a proven authority in matters of fact has become, after 300 years of success in science and technology, a matter of common sense. Consequently it is much harder to criticize and to replace. Nonetheless a close examination shows that experience will not do, either. Here are three devastating arguments against the theory that experience should be regarded as a final and authoritative arbiter on matters of fact:

1. Experience cannot tell us that what we take to be the laws of nature will not alter in the future (say, tonight).
2. Experience is insufficient warrant for a statement reporting experience, since we may be deluded, dreaming, drunk, or simply mistaken in our judgement of what we experienced (Descartes).
3. No universal statement is ever proved by the accumulation of particular statements which are instances of it (unless the instances exhaust the possibilities) (Aristotle).

Let us put these objections another way. Three steps are required for experience to prove scientific theories to be true:

(*i*) Experience (*E*) has to warrant observation reports (*O*):

(*ii*) Observation reports have to warrant laws as we think them to be (*L*).

(*iii*) The laws (L) have to be identified with true laws of nature (*T*).

Since members of *L* are intended to be invariant over time and space but members of *T* may not be, the third step is not justified even if the first two are. It is an ontological problem whether the universe persists with the same behaviour patterns. Traditionally, believers in a powerful deity have argued for the view that the deity is free not only to intervene in a manner which does not violate *T* (naturalist theory of miracles), nor only, in addition, to intervene in a manner which does violate T, but also he is free to alter *T*, say to *T'*. But belief in a powerful deity is not a necessary condition for belief in the possibility that *T* may alter.

Usually we set Maimonides' objection aside. In doing so, we may say that though our aim may be to improve *L* so that it approximates *T* more closely, the only way we can do this is to aim for a version of *L* justified by *O* which in turn has been justified by *E*; if *T* alters (to *T'*) then in time *E* will alter to *E'* and *O* to *O'*; in our efforts to explain *O'*, we should change *L* to *L'* hopefully approximating *T'*. But we should be wrong in replying to Maimonides this way. If we changed *L* to *L'* because of changes in *E* and *O* subsequent upon altering *T*, *L'* would not be approximating *T'* so much as a superordinate set of laws *T** of which T and *T'* were special cases, since in inventing *L* we would be trying to accommodate *both* E and *E'* in laws that were invariant with respect to time and space. Hence we should never notice if the true laws of nature changed, since the resultant changes in *E* would be indistinguishable from those we might have expected if *L* was still only a poor approximation to *T*. We would mistakenly think of *L'* as a better approximation to *T*. Nonetheless, for the sake of progress in science, we do set Maimonides' objection aside. This should perhaps be regarded as a *methodological* decision: it sets one of the rules for science.

Descartes's objection has received much more attention from philosophers in modern times than has Maimonides'. Even so, it is usually ignored by scientists who agree that if enough of us do research and check each other's results we can overcome the risk of being mistaken in reporting what we observe, at least on the macroscopic scale. This is a pragmatically sufficient rejoinder to DESCARTES'S objections and it has led to recent lack of interest among philosophers in the problems of the empirical basis of science. Nonetheless, it is not a sufficient rejoinder to another version of Descartes's objection, a version raised by Popper, namely that since all observational terms are general terms they are theory-laden. Now, if theories are to be proved by induction from experience, all inductive proofs (if there be any) will suffer from a mild attack of *petitio principii*. (Recently, a similar point has been made by Goodman.) The importance of the problem lies here: the names used in theories in science indicate classes, thus dividing objects in the real world into these classes. Perhaps the divisions thus rendered are natural, perhaps not. Complacency over terminology may lead to stagnation, while a lively sense of the possible inadequacy of the classification produced by physical theory may encourage criticism and improved conjecture. Thus in this respect

$$M_2 \xrightarrow{r} P_2$$

and possibly also

$$M_2 \xrightarrow{r} P_1 .$$

Aristotle's objection, which is repeated by Hume (whose presentation confuses it with Maimonides'), cannot be at all easily set aside. There clearly are logical relations of deducibility between observational (particular) data and general laws: laws entail data; some data refute laws. In symbols:

if $(x)_A\,(Fx)$ and $a \in A$ then $F\,a$;

and

if $b \in A$ and $\sim F\,b$ then $\sim(x)_A\,(Fx)$.

On the other hand, the inductive relation is less firm:

$(x)_A\,(Fx)$

is *not* entailed by:

$Fa \,\&\, Fb \,\&\, Fc \,\&\, Fd\ldots$ (where $a, b, c, d\ldots \in A$)

unless the class A is exhausted by the instances cited.

The situation is perhaps even worse than this, since, as Duhem pointed out long ago, there is an infinite number of mathematical functions which "fit" any finite number of observation reports. He thought this introduced considerable arbitrariness into the construction of physical theory. With the admission of the failure of full justification of scientific laws, it was natural, we suppose, that philosophers and scientists should look for as strong a justification as possible. Despite Hume's arguments against trying even to probability laws, some interpretation of the Probability Calculus was sought (and in some now dwindling circles, still is) under which there could be measured the degree of confirmation an hypothesis gained on certain evidence. Many philosophers saw the power of negative instances in refuting generalities, contrasted to the ineffectiveness of positive instances (even of varied kinds) in lending support, but the first to propose criticism (refutation) as the key to the non-arbitrariness of hypotheses in science was Popper. Popper correctly saw that confirmation or justification, in the sense of the accumulation and parade of positive instances, did not distinguish science from pseudoscience. He proposed that empirical falsifiability be the criterion for the scientific status of strictly universal sentences (laws); and he further proposed that science could be distinguished from non science (especially pseudo-science) by a *critical policy*, the policy of submitting our hypotheses to servere testing in the hope of uncovering their faults.

The proposal of Popper's, to give up trying to justify laws and to try to refute them instead, is so revolutionary it seems sometimes not to be understood even by some of his admirers. For instance, Lakatos appears to think failure to refute equals partial justification. Popper's philosophical opponents certainly do not comprehend his proposal which is not surprising, since it would impose a radically different programme of research upon philosophers and even upon scientists. Traditionally, in epistemology, philosophers have sought a formula for showing that this or that method of arguing or of introducing evidence, or this or that authority or source of information, was the proper mode or source to use in establishing what was being claimed, so that all reasonable men would be *obliged* to concur. This happy formula has never been found. In its place, Popper has proposed critical debate. An old enough suggestion, to be sure. "Back to the Presocratics", indeed! Everyone knows one must use critical debate. Popper's proposal however goes much further than is customary. His proposal is not simply to use critical debate as a prolegomenon to proof, as a way of dealing with the opposition before establishing one's own position, but rather as the whole mode of inquiry. Traditionally, knowledge has been viewed as justified true belief; Popper proposes to view it as not yet-refuted, possibly false, conjecture.

The relevance for physics of the debate over epistemology need hardly be argued: P_1 includes observational reports, empirical laws, and theories which have passed some criterion of adequacy, else just any report or putative law would be included; epistemology is the study of some of these criteria of adequacy. Shall we include in P_1 only those statements for which we can give warrant, and if so, how strict is our notion of warrant? Or shall we, on the other hand, include theories which, although we cannot give them warrant, nonetheless satisfy the criterion of explaining certain puzzles, or solving certain problems, to which experience has given rise? When (if ever) shall we remove an erstwhile satisfactory theory from P_1 and on what grounds? These questions are specific variants of the central epistemological question and they clearly are relevant to physics, at least because varying answers may vary the content of P_1. Hence, again,

$$M_2 \xrightarrow{r} P_1$$

as well as

$$M_2 \xrightarrow{r} P_2 .$$

What should we now say about the credence to be placed in claims about the existence of occult entities or qualities? Rejection of the occult, either hidden properties of visible things, or hidden things, follows from the requirement to justify knowledge empirically. In modern times it seems to have been thought that a necessary condition for the adoption of occult entities or qualities is the rejection of empiricism. This is not so. The rejection of the requirement to justify knowledge is sufficient to liberate us to adopt hypotheses or theories positing the occult. The rejection of the requirement to justify scientific knowledge empirically might, however, be thought to threaten the empirical basis of science, since traditionally this has been thought to be secured by the mass of empirical evidence in favour of the laws and theories of science. Popper has suggested the alternative that the empirical basis of science is secured by the empirical testability of scientific laws. Hence occult entities or qualities may be admitted, if hypotheses about them could be rendered testable, even if only indirectly. In my view, we may go even further, taking our cue from Popper's definition of the aim of science: "to find satisfactory explanations of whatever strikes us as being in need of an explanation", and say that occult entities and qualities may be properly introduced into scientific discourse if they help explain what we think needs explaining. The general requirement that we hold our explanations open to criticism (including empirical criticisms, if any can be devised) is, it seems to me, a sufficient constraint upon arbitrariness.

Perhaps it is only a question of emphasis, perhaps it is more fundamental, that Popper's view shifts our attention from support to explanation. Logically these are complementary: generalities explain instances, instances support generalities. we suspect the shift is of some importance, however, not only logically since explanation is deductive while support is inductive, but also methodologically since a stress upon explanation will encourage growth of knowledge by encouraging improvement in explanations while a stress on support will discourage growth by encouraging

$$M_2 \xrightarrow{r} P_1$$

entrenchment. Hence, again and

$$M_2 \xrightarrow{r} P_2$$

Methodology, Logic and Axiology

The methodological question, How do we learn what there is to know?, cannot be separated from questions in the logic, ethics and aesthetics of science, since methodology studies the means by which certain ends are sought: the means are supposed to be rational, hence logical considerations enter; and any consideration of ends and means implies value theory. This is especially the case in view of the discussion in previous sections. Let me elaborate.

In the days when it was assumed that truth was easy to come by, that thorough justification could be given for knowledge, and that anybody who applied himself diligently might learn all there was to know (or at least, all there was that was worth knowing) it was plausible to suppose that knowing was beneficial. Hence, scientific inquiry justified itself by its success. Nowadays all these assumptions are questioned, as is even the criterion of success. There is too much to know for one man to know all, hence he must choose in which area to seek education and to prosecute research. This raises any number of moral and aesthetic considerations for the individual. Furthermore, knowledge is not thought now to be incorrigible. It may even be somewhat elusive. Justification of a thorough kind cannot be given for theoretical knowledge, though we may say why we think we are right. (Incidentally, the less precise and the less general our knowledge is, the more firm it may be regarded, which is why refuted theories such as Newton's gravitational theory or Boyle's Law are firmly entrenched once the limits within which they are held to apply are established. Any theory at all may be established by weakening the demands of accuracy, and any theory refuted by strengthening them.) Saying why we think we are right amounts to explaining how the knowledge we claim to have satisfies certain desiderata. Perhaps in addition we might try to say why these particular desiderata (or criteria of admission to P_1), and not some others, ought to be satisfied. In the nature of the case, then, decisions to include or exclude an hypothesis will have an aesthetic and even a moral component. That some lines of research are more obviously beneficial to mankind, if successfully pursued, than others enhances the importance of the moral component.

Let us assume that the quest for truth (or for knowledge, as an approximation to truth) is worth prosecuting, though we may have reservations about whether searching for just *any* knowledge is worth the cost. Then we may ask what criteria we shall set up for judging whether a certain hypothesis is preferable as an approximation to the truth than a rival; and we may ask by what means we might seek even more satisfactory hypotheses. We may also ask what the criteria are which an hypothesis must satisfy for us even to entertain it as a possibility. The answers to these questions will pick out a methodology. Here are a few answers:

In physics, we do not entertain hypotheses which explain nothing.

We count on explanation E_1 of an event e_1 as satisfactory in an elementary fashion if e_1 is implied by E_1, though perhaps not directly. For example: $(x)_A\,(F_x)$ explains F_a, if $a \in A$.

We count E_1 better than E_2 if E_1 explains all that E_2 explains and, in addition, explains some events E_2 does not explain, especially if E_1 explains events which clash with E_2.

Examples of other desiderata are elegance, simplicity, consistency, and exactness. A requirement which is frequently effective (usually implicitly), and which may be seriously questioned as to its propriety, is agreement with a world-view. Perhaps our hope of improving our world-view lies in seriously entertaining hypotheses which challenge it.

Just as there can be no thoroughly justified scientific knowledge so, analogously, there cannot be any self-evident aesthetic and moral criteria by which to settle disputes as to which hypotheses to entertain, which to adopt, and so on. What characteristics a theory of physics should possess is not immediately obvious. Various champions of various philosophical (religious or atheistic) causes have proposed varieties of sets of characteristics. At root the debate may be ontological: it may be a debate about the characteristics of the universe in general, and hence the characteristics any putative description of the world should have. For example, if there is no objective chance, laws must be deterministic rather than statistical. On the other hand, if the aim of inquiry is thought to be the facilitation of prediction and control of the future, ease of computation and closeness of fit to data will be prime desiderata. And so on. On the surface, however, the debate concerns what features we prefer theories to possess, and consequently, the considerations are aesthetic. Popper has stressed the conventional character of methodological decisions; and AGASSI has stressed the institutional context of the debate, and subsequent decisions. We wish here to stress the aesthetic and moral quality of the desiderata and hence of the decisions. Even should there be a consensus within the scientific community over which desiderata to use and which hypotheses to choose as a result, this would not remove the aesthetic and moral dimension. Incidentally it is unlikely that we could get a general consensus as to the boundaries of the scientific community all pseudo-scientists as well as all scientists would no doubt wish to draw the boundary so as to include themselves, and until the boundary is drawn we do not know whom to count as competent, as a scientist, to draw it. Vicious circle! Perhaps we should recognize that quite private sets of preferences may motivate the research interest of and the criteria of acceptability used by, individual scientists. Debate between scientists protects the community from arbitrariness but not from (sometimes acrimonious) dispute.

Considerable work has been done in the literature to analyze some of the desiderata. And this is to be welcomed, provided it is not part of a general programme to eliminate aesthetic and moral considerations. Such a programme would be misguided, since, although these considerations may be taken for granted or ignored, they cannot be eliminated. Worse, it would be mischievous, since, without openness there would likely be no criticism; and without criticism errors have too good a chance to be perpetuated — methodological errors as much as errors in theory. On the other hand, a scrutiny of the desiderata that are or may be or (perhaps) should be used, the scrutiny not necessarily including an analysis, in case the desideratum is simple or primitive, but definitely including a comparison of the likely outcomes of the use or non-use of the various desiderata, would improve the chances of the desiderata being appropriate and enhance the competence with which they were used. Hence

$$M_5 \xrightarrow{r} P_1$$

and

$$M_5 \xrightarrow{r} P_2 .$$

Such a scrutiny would also supply us with a much needed theory of success to replace the traditional, but refuted, theory that success is being right or very nearly right.

The moral considerations arise mostly from a clash between the interest of individual scientists (and even of groups of scientists) on the one hand and the interests of society in general on the other. This clash is a recent phenomenon: only recently has large scale public funding been made available to science for teaching and research; and only recently have the outcomes of research (in the shape of technological innovations) been recognized so widely as potentially destructive of the quality of life and even of life itself. It is not surprising, then, that the modern image of the scientist as a lonely research worker pursuing truth for its own sake, financed by himself or by some lay benefactor has to be changed. Society has too many pressing problems requiring solutions for it to tolerate the expenditure of all its research funds on projects which match the research interests and curiosity of individual scientists without having any foreseeable beneficial consequences for society as a whole. There is a strong moral case for scientists choosing research problems which relate to social problems and social goals. In this way, moral considerations might influence physics in all its aspects. Clearly if aesthetic and moral considerations are relevant to physics, the study of value as such (value theory in its generic sense) is relevant also. Hence,

$$M_5 \xrightarrow{r} P.$$

Now for some remarks about logic.

The virtues of axiomatization of physical theory have been "preached" persuasively, as well as demonstrated in practice, by Bunge. We concur with his conclusion that exposing the deductively related core of a theory is beneficial to physics, bringing conceptual clarity, stimulating criticism and hence promoting growth of knowledge. Hence

$$M_4 \xrightarrow{r} P_1.$$

Similarly, benefit accrues from exposing the deductive logical relations between theories, empirical laws and specific consequences of these. The methodology of science is clearer when the arguments used in criticism are sharpened in focus. For example, it was assumed by many philosophers that negative instances counted in a straightforward fashion against generalities. Duhem seems to have been the first to point out that a battery of assumptions is needed to augment a physical theory before testable consequences may be deduced from it, hence the falsification of a prediction entails the falsity of the conjunction of many assumptions rather than the falsity of any one.

A decision is required as to which of the assumptions to take as falsified. A very clear presentation of normal scientific practice, from which, no doubt, there are well argued exceptions, has been given recently by Bunge. We am in favour of an attempt to state what current practice is. This is too frequently ignored by philosophers who address themselves to science as a logical possibility rather than a social phenomenon. Nonetheless, it is appropriate for us to note that, since the considerations which lead to decisions of the kind we are here concerned with are ontological and aesthetic (and perhaps even moral) it might be beneficial to science for this not to be concealed.

By contrast with the fruits of axiomatization, the anticipated fruits were not born of the labours to provide a logic of *induction*. Much was gained by way of clarification of side issues, but the central task of providing an algorism for computing the degree to which an hypothesis was supported by evidence or at least of providing an analysis of the notion of degree of support (or confirmation) appears to be futile. Nevertheless the language of support, the language of a justificationist theory of the relation of evidence to hypothesis is, regrettably, common parlance among scientists. Logical analysis has not yet had its full impact upon the modes of speech, and hence, one might guess, upon the research styles and aims, of many scientists.

In my view, the only tenable theories of method are those which prescribe critical debate not only of theories but also of the desiderata they are supposed to satisfy and which stress the logical connections between the various constituents of P_1. From the unsatisfactory methodology of Bacon we may borrow the notion of experience supplying us both with problems and with criticisms of theories. From the unsatisfactory methodology of Descartes we may borrow the notion of the intellect supplying general concepts and hypotheses to explain experience. Thus what were originally seen as authorities to bind our allegiance (experience and the intellect) are now to be viewed as sources of (corrigible) knowledge, held open to criticism. Science is sometimes represented as a sophisticated version of learning from experience, but this unbalances the mixture. In science we learn not only from experience but also from intuition: the various desiderata which we oblige physical theory to satisfy are not found in the phenomena, but are imposed upon them by us. Provided such imposition is done critically, it is not improper. These methodological considerations are clearly relevant to physics as a discipline:

$$M_3 \xrightarrow{r} P_2 .$$

We conjecture that a critical methodology used by a competent scientist, with ordinary luck in his research, will improve the body of knowledge:

$$M_3 \xrightarrow{r} P_1 .$$

Summary

An analysis of philosophy and a scrutiny of its parts leads us to the view that the study of a quite broad variety of philosophical problems not only is relevant to physics but also may be beneficial to physics as a body of knowledge, as a discipline and as a social institution.

□□□

11

Future Changes in Theoretical Physics

Introduction

A number of philosophers have called our attention to what they claim to be more far-reaching types of theoretical revision. Not only the factual content but also the very meaning of the expressions used in a theory are subject to revision. The theoretician may introduce new concepts, that is new expressions with new meaning, as well as revise concepts already in use.

Some philosophers have claimed or implicitly assumed that all theoretical revisions amount to conceptual changes. The rejection of any distinction between conceptual and factual change has led them to reject a number of tenets central to what is generally called empiricism and realism. These tenets include the belief that observational evidence is methodologically relevant to the acceptance and rejection of theories, that distinct theories can be compared in regard to their relative value, and that distinct theories can be formulated about the same objects.

We have no doubt that there are episodes in the history of science in which new concepts are introduced or old expressions are given new meanings, and new expressions with new meanings are used profitably for the first time. Yet we believe that criteria for diagnosing conceptual changes and the logical and methodological import of such changes have yet to be adequately specified. In what follows we will attempt to (1) specify what does and what does not serve as a useful indicator or criterion of conceptual change (2) show that conceptual change can be and often is a matter of gradual evolution via discrete episodes rather than complete replacement (3) make, clarify and defend the claim that conceptual change is a change (not necessarily an improvement) in the capacities of individuals or groups for conducting research in contrast to a change in the results of exercising these capacities. I believe that my contribution to the completion of these tasks should help to appropriately clarify and qualify the above tenets of empiricism, which we regard as incontrovertible but unclear.

Criteria for Meaning and for Meaning-Change

One is tempted to say that episodes in which the concepts of a given field are revised or completely replaced can be identified by the introduction of symbols hitherto not appearing in sentences expressing observations and theories of the field.

Semantical rules, e.g., '"*F*" designates force,' '"*p*" can be used to refer to one of the set of protons *P*', are also of little use in diagnosing conceptual selection or change. The rules cannot be understood unless the observer of scientific development appreciates the conception of force and proton intended in these statements. However, the possibility of equivocation applies equally to expressions used in stating semantical rules as to expressions used in stating the laws and principles of a theory. 'Force' in the rule might have any of the several meanings that '*F*' might have in the several actual theories using this expression.

The above-mentioned semantical rules are generally taken as conventional meta theoretical statements, for the expression-types mentioned (and not used) in them (*F*, *p*, etc.) are arbitrarily selected for correlation with extra-theoretical objects or concepts. Some writers have distinguished *semantical assumptions* from semantical rules, claiming that the assumptions are not conventional but are proper hypotheses that might be false. We can concede this distinction with this proviso: In *theoretical frameworks* such as classical particle or quantum mechanics or relativistic particle mechanics, the semantical assumptions are general existential and not singular statements.

For example, classical particle mechanics contains as a proper axiom the equivalent sentences $\Sigma \neq \Lambda$ or $(\exists x)(x \in \Sigma)$, which, in view of semantical rules for 'Σ', can be interpreted as 'The set of material particles is not empty,' or 'There exists a material object.' Similarly, fundamental particle theories should contain '$P \neq \Lambda$' or its equivalent as a proper axiom. The latter axiom allows us to take the rule '"*pi*" (*i*=1, ... , *n*) can be used to refer to a proton' as granting permission for the referential use of n individual names '*pi*' (*i*=1, ... , *n*) or of the singular descriptions *ιx* ($x \in P$ & ... *i*...), where the ... *i*... is to be filled with a singular proposition specifying the spatiotemporal extent of the *i*-th particle p_i.

Nevertheless, both the semantical rule and the assumption it presupposes can be used equivocally, and hence their appearance among axioms and meta statements of two different theories is not sufficient to justify the claim that '*P*' and 'p_i' mean the same in their occurrences in the two theories.

It is widely held that a necessary condition for two expressions having the same meaning is that one expression can be substituted for one other in a logically or analytically true sentence so as to preserve the necessary truth of that sentence. Accordingly, if the necessary truth of a sentence is not preserved under such substitution, we may conclude that the expressions used in the substitution differ in meaning. However, this relation between sameness of meaning and substitutivity cannot be used as a criterion for meaning change in scientific development because substitutivity is one of the questions at issue in determining how two different theories might be compared. That is, in comparing two theories, T_1, and T_2, an item of interest is whether statements and arguments in T_1, can be paraphrased by statements and arguments in T_2. In other words, can expressions in T_1 be substituted for similar expressions in statements and arguments in T_2 without altering the validity of these arguments or the truth of these statements? Substitutivity as a criterion for meaning change simply begs this important question.

The syntax of a theory's non-logical expressions is relevant to but insufficient for determining uniquely the concepts designated by these expressions, as we shall see below. One theory might construe 'mass' as a property, and another might construe it as a relation. However, any particular theory might mention several properties or relations, so that within a theory specification of an expression's syntactical properties leaves open the possibility of equivocation. *A fortiori*, if the expression '*M*' is characterized as a predicate in one theory and a relation in the other, it does not follow that the same concept '*M*' is revised in going from one to the other theory. '*M*' might be used to designate mass in one and force in the other theory, two completely distinct concepts.

Semantical rules of the kind so far considered are usually advanced in order to specify the *extension, denotation* or *reference* of the nonlogical expressions used in a theory. However, most students of semantics are aware that these concepts do not capture all of an expression's 'meaning,' for expressions can be co-extensive or co-referring and yet 'mean' quite different things, e.g., 'the author of *Waverly*' and 'Sir Walter Scott,' or 'rational animal' and 'extant featherless biped.' Accordingly, it is commonplace to distinguish an expression's sense or intension from its reference or extension. Meaning then is construed as determined by both the sense and reference of an expression in a manner expressed by, e.g., the formula *M(X, CM)*= <*S(X, CM)*, *R(X, CM)*>, where '*M (X, CM)*' abbreviates 'the meaning of expression X in classical mechanics,' '*S(X, CM)*' is 'the sense of *X* in classical mechanics,' and '*R(X, CM)*' is 'the reference of *X* in classical mechanics.'

In what follows I will be concerned with specifying those components (statements or hypotheses) of a theory that determine the sense of that theory's non-logical expressions. A change in these components is necessary and sufficient for a shift in the sense of the relevant expression, and consequently such a change is sufficient for a shift in that expression's meaning.

I propose that a satisfactorily enriched statement of any given theory should be accompanied with statements the understanding and assent to which is necessary and sufficient for ascribing capacities for conducting research within that framework. These statements determine the sense of the extralogical expressions used in that framework. In the case studies below, I will try to show that these statements, criterial statements, provide logical links between these and other like expressions and between these expressions and expressions already in use either in other theories or in ordinary language supported by a background of commonsense beliefs.

The criterial statements can, but need not, specify both conditions fully justifying a theoretical term's application (sufficient conditions) and conditions the failure of which fully justifies the denial of its application (necessary conditions). That is, a criterial statement might be phrased 'For all x, x has mass if and only if P_1 x and P_2 x and $P_n x$.' (P_1, ..., P_n stand for the specified criteria.) It might also, but need not, specify conditions that are jointly necessary but individually sufficient. That is, the criterion might be phrased 'For all x, x has mass if P_1 x or P_2 x or ... or $P_n x$, and

x has mass only if P_1 x and P_2 x and ... and $P_n x$.' Further alternatives might include the specification of any number of the P_1, ..., P_n as individually or jointly necessary and any number of the same list, and not necessarily including any necessary conditions, as individually or jointly sufficient conditions. For example, our criterion might be 'For all x, x has mass if P_1 x and P_2 x and only if P_4 x or P_5 x or P_6 x'.

The properties. P_1, ..., P_n need not be directly observable. That is, they need not be properties for which there are epistemic standards of the form 'a would not look (taste, feel, smell, sound, etc.) L under conditions C unless it were P_i'. A property P_i could also be linked to directly observable properties by physical law, or for the present there may be no known laws linking P_i to such properties.

2. An Example: Criteria for "... has Mass"

That an object is seen, felt, heard, tasted or smelled are individually sufficient conditions for ascribing mass. In fact, the weaker conditions of visibility, tangibility, etc., are sufficient conditions for attributing that quality. The list of alternative sufficient conditions is extended in physics to include properties of microphysical objects that cannot be directly observed, e.g., a macrophysical object's being capable of capture or bottling (Lavoisier's or Hero of Alexandria's 'gases' or 'airs') a microphysical object's possessing weight or possessing less than maximal velocity of light in relativistic kinematics.

The last mentioned of the above conditions is necessary for an object's having classical or relativistic mass. However, we believe that this condition was not widely recognized in classical mechanics before the advent of the special theory of relativity, for there were surely pre-relativistic physicists willing to contemplate infinite velocities generated by infinite forces in finite masses or infinite velocities in infinite time, generated by finite forces. Rather, most of the various attempts to 'define' classical mass take the capacity for exerting an impulse or (equivalently) for transferring momentum as a necessary condition for the possession of mass. This aspect of the concept of mass was revised after the relativistic account of radiation pressure appeared.

The sufficient conditions mentioned above are always *logically relevant* but are *useful* for deciding application of 'has mass' under some but not under all circumstances. Massive objects are visible only under certain conditions, and many of these conditions are common knowledge that can be explained by the laws of wave-optics and the anatomy and physiology of our visual receptors. In the light of this knowledge, an object's having been seen is a useful criterion for the application of has mass' if conditions of visibility exist or can be produced artifically. Our technical shortcomings can affect the utility but not the logical relevance of a criterion. Accordingly, if we cannot weigh electrons, weight is not a useful sufficient condition for ascribing mass to them. However, the invention of the appropriate instrument or techniques or the formulation or application of laws relating electron mass to technically observable properties can make the logically relevant quality weight a useful sufficient condition for calling electrons material objects.

The more extended a list of logically relevant conditions we have, the wider the range of objects that fall into the scope of our activities of ascribing mass. Also, the greater our awareness of the utility of criteria already known to be logically relevant, the more deliberate will be our actions of determining whether mass ought to be ascribed. That is, we may select in advance criteria known to be useful rather than randomly trying to evaluate all properties, whether logically relevant or useful. Accordingly, one can sharpen his conception of mass by acquiring knowledge of the community's technological capacities, and the community can extend its capabilities in attributing mass by advancing the technology relevant to evaluating properties logically relevant to 'has mass'.

Note that on this analysis we can conceive of mass in domains in which we lack the technical capacity or useful criteria for its application. Thus, 'A proton at the Sun's centre has mass' is a cognitively meaningful sentence.

Background and Theory-Specific Criteria

In the preceding section criteria for 'has mass' have been stated in two different ways. They are phrased in general and perhaps vague terms including 'visible', 'tangible', and 'incapable of maximal velocity'. These we might call statements of *background criteria*. They are also stated in forms making them specific to the theories mentioned, pre-classical, classical and relativistic mechanics. The latter statements are patently less general and perhaps less vague, and might be called *theory specific criteria*. The distinction between these two types of criteria help us to understand several features of conceptual development, whether in the individual or in the community.

In the first place, it is in the light of background criteria and shared beliefs or conceptions that we may determine whether two theories are mutually *contradictories, contraries* or *subcontraries*. Theories *T* and *T'* are contradictories if the truth of the first entails the falsity of the second, the falsity of the first entails the truth of the second, and, conversely, the falsity of the second entails the truth of the first and the truth of the second entails the falsity of the first. *T* and *T'* are contraries if the truth of the first entails the falsity of the second and the truth of the second entails the falsity of the first, but the falsity of neither entails the truth of the other. *T* and *T'* are subcontraries if the falsity of the first entails the truth of the second and the falsity of the second entails the truth of the first, but the truth of neither entails the falsity of the other. Let us consider two scientists, S_1 and S_2, who agree that they are studying the same object, a. Suppose also that S_1 believes that this object has mass, and his belief can be expressed by the sentence M^1a. Also, S_2 believes that it is not the case that a has mass, or - *Ma*.

(The superscripts here and in what follows identify the vocabulary, S_1's or S_2's vocabulary, in which the predicate occurs.) Furthermore, S_1 subscribes to criteria which can be stated thus:

$$P_1^1$$

is sufficient for the application of M^1 or

$$(x)(P_1^1x \Rightarrow M^1x),$$

and

$$P_2^1$$

is necessary for M^1's application, or

$$(x)(-P_2^1x \Rightarrow M^1x).$$

S_2 subscribes to criteria stated as

$$(x)(P_1^2x \Rightarrow M^2x)$$

and

$$(x)(-P_2^2x \Rightarrow -M^2x)$$

On the basis of these criteria the following cases provide sufficient, and in some cases, minimal conditions for S_1's and S_2's theories being (1) complementary, (2) sub-contrary, (3) contrary and (4) contradictory:

1. M^1 a and -M^2 a are complementary on the basis of the above criteria if the conjoined statements

$$'P_1^1\ a \ \&\ -P_2^2\ a'$$

and

$$'-P_2^1\ \&\ P_1^2a'$$

each represent a possible state of affairs. Under the stated criteria, the first statement entails that both M^1 a and -M^2 a are true and the second entails that they both are false.

Note also, if

$P_1^1\ a$

or

$-P_2^1\ a$

or

$-P_2^1\ a$

or

$-P_2^2\ a$

'does not represent a technically or physically possible state of affairs, S_1's and S_2's theories are methodologically incommensurable with respect to the given criteria. That is, the criteria link their theories with no possible states of affairs that would warrant the acceptance or rejection of one in the light of some or no evidence for or against the other.

2. S_1's and S_2's claims are sub-contraries if and only if for any object a,

$P_2^2\ a$

and

$-P_1^1\ a$

cannot both be true. Now, if S_1 and S_2 share the belief that

$P_2^2\ a$

implies

$P_1^1\ a$,

then either $M^1 a$, or $-M^2 a$, or perhaps both, are true. A fortiori, if S_1 and S_2 conceive

P_1^1

and

P_2^2

in their background beliefs as the same property, their theories are subcontraries.

3. $M^1 a$ and $-M^2 a$ are contraries if S_1 and S_2 agree at least that

$P_2^1 a$

implies

$P_1^2 a$.

A fortiori, if they identify these properties in their background beliefs, both of their theories cannot be true.

4. If S_1 and S_2 agree that

$P_2^2 a$

implies

$P_1^1 a$

and

$P_2^1 a$

implies

$P_1^2 a$,

then $M^1 a$ and $-M^2 a$ cannot both be true and cannot both be false. These are minimal conditions for the two theories being contradictories. Again, the stronger condition that

P_1^1

and

P_2^2,

and

$$P_1^2$$

and

$$P_2^1$$

are respectively identical also entails that the two theories are contradictories.

We can also appeal to the distinction between theory-specific and background criteria for clarification of the commonplace claim that a new theory can further clarify a concept already current is scientific or everyday thought. Classical continuum and particle mechanics contains considerable elaboration and refinement of the pre-classical 'change in condition,' the effects of forces. Relativistic particle mechanics offered an alternative specification to the classical notion of maximal velocity. Insofar as puzzles about infinite forces and velocities were unresolved in classical particle mechanics, relativity can be viewed as containing a positive contribution to the clarity of this concept and the related concept of mass.

The theory-specific criteria stand and fall with the theory to which they are characteristic and peculiar. The change or the further specification of such criteria are one factor constituting conceptual change in the development of scientific ideas.

Yet there remain 'analytic truths' which might not be changed in some or perhaps all episodes of the development of a given concept, and these are expressed in the background criteria. By means of these background beliefs or conceptions we may determine what, if any, logical relations are borne by theories that differ in their conceptual content. We can also distinguish between conceptual revision and total conceptual innovation or replacement. In the latter case the criteria and shared background beliefs are insufficient to establish any logical relations of contrarity, contradictoriness, etc. between the theories, leaving them complementary or perhaps even methodologically incommensurable.

Syntactical Axioms

Modifying the syntactical characteristics of an expression is relevant to conceptual change but not sufficient for diagnosing such change. An axiomatic statement of a theory, such as classical particle mechanics, non-relativistic quantum mechanics, or classical electromagnetic field theory, should contain among its axioms a number of statements characterizing the nonlogical vocabulary of that theory. These statements, *syntactical axioms*, specify which elements of that vocabulary are predicates, relations, singular terms and functions. They also specify sets of objects over which these expressions are defined. They specify expressions which, when appropriately juxtaposed with certain symbols for the nonlogical expressions, generate further terms or propositions.

For example, an axiomatization of classical particle mechanics might contain statements such as the following:

Every *material particle* has a unique positive real-valued mass. Symbolically, this statement may be expressed in the form

$M: \Sigma \rightarrow R+$

which says 'M is a function from the set Σ of material objects onto the set $R+$ of positive real numbers.' Similarly, force is characterized as follows:

Internal force is a vector-valued quantity defined for material particle pairs.

In symbolic terms, $F: \Sigma \times \Sigma \rightarrow R^3$. That is, F is a function from the cartesian product of sets of material particles $\Sigma 2$ onto a real vector space R^3.

Once we have a conceptual background in which 'material particle,' 'time interval of duration Δt,' 'spatial interval of length Δs,' 'interval on the set of real numbers R,' etc., are understood, these axioms characterize sharply the distinct quantities force and mass. 'Material particle' can be characterized in a general way by reference to criteria for 'has mass.' 'Time interval of duration Δt' is characterized in terms of an antecedently understood chronology and chronometry, wherein there appear criteria of varying degrees of generality similar to those described for 'mass'. Topology and geometry are similarly appealed to for spatial intervals. Finally 'real number interval R,' etc., are understood in terms of the formal or logical background of the theory.

With this background, the above axioms capture several important aspects of the technical and quantitative concepts of mass and force appearing within the classical framework. Mass is construed as a scalar quantity that can take on only positive values. Force, on the other hand, is a vector. That is, direction as well as magnitude is relevant to specifying force-values, and forces can be resolved into components in any direction in space. Mass is an intrinsic property of all material particles in the classical framework, whereas force-values depend upon attributes of material particle pairs.

In the special theory of relativity an object's mass is dependent upon velocity, where velocity must be specified in relation to a specific inertial frame of reference. Accordingly, an object's mass must be specified with respect to an inertial frame. The classical syntactical axiom for mass then is revised to read:

Every material object in relation to a specific inertial frame has a unique positive real-valued mass.

Thus, in the framework of special relativity mass is a relational and not an intrinsic quality.

Pragmatic Import

Three factors are relevant to the conceptual content of a theory and must be specified in any complete account of the sense of the non-logical terms of a theory. I have mentioned the criterial statements and the syntactical axioms in which a given expression is characterized. A third factor that I have not mentioned is the overall selection of extra-logical expressions used in a given theory, syntactical axioms and criterial statements. For example, '... has mass' may appear in the extra logical vocabulary of one but not of another theory. I will now attempt to relate these factors in terms of their bearing upon the capacities of individual researchers, viz. their bearing upon strategies and techniques that facilitate, but are not necessary or sufficient for, successful empirical investigation and theory formation.

The overall selection of non-logical expressions in a given theory represents a belief on the part of a proponent of that theory regarding which properties, relations and quantities are relevant to the objectives of research within that theory. For example, we might suppose that one objective of research in classical particle mechanics is the explanation of the behavior of macroscopic material systems such as pendulums, planets, and vibrating strings. The selection of vocabulary for classical particle mechanics constitutes a commitment to the view that an empirical evaluation of the number of particulate components of a system, their masses, initial positions and velocities and their interactions, will contribute to the achievement of this objective. On the other hand, the determination of their color, taste, or perhaps their chemical constitution is held to be far less, if at all, likely to contribute to the explanation of their behavior.

This selection of terms not only directs an investigator to look for specific properties, relations and quantities, but also sets specific limitations within which these properties, etc., can occur. That is, one who subscribes to the syntactical axioms of classical particle mechanics holds the view in advance of any empirical investigation that an object's mass will never be less than zero and can always be represented by a unique positive real number. Similarly, a force must have a specific direction in space as well as a unique real magnitude. Masses of individual particles also are not expected to change in time or with any other mechanical attribute, but forces may vary in time according to specific parameters describing the conditions of interacting objects.

By contrast, a researcher acting in accordance with the syntactical axioms of special relativity believes that he must specify an inertial frame before asking for a unique answer to 'What is the mass of object a?' It is thus that the direction of research under the special theory differs from that under classical particle mechanics. Yet the difference is not total, for background criteria shared by the two theories entail that the question is relevant in the same general circumstances, e. g., when confronted with a visible object, one that is not moving with maximal velocity, etc.

Our capacities for carrying out empirical research can be ordered with regard to the relation '... is a prerequisite for ...'. For example, before one can appreciate the fact that the application of '... has mass' constitutes a problem for empirical research, he must believe that the predicate applies in some but not in other circumstances. Also a prerequisite for the problem of evaluating quantitatively the mass of an object is that the qualitative predicate '... has mass' be correctly applied. Accordingly, one must understand and assent to some of the criteria peculiar to '... has mass' (as distinct from other contingent predicates '... is colored,' etc.), viz. one or more of the sufficient conditions for its application, before he can deliberately act in the application of that predicate and, *a fortiori*, before he can legitimately raise a question regarding its quantity. Similarly, an investigator must understand and assent to criteria for the relations '... is greater in mass than ...' and '... is equal in mass to ...' before considering problems such as 'How much greater in mass is σ than σ' ?'.

This ordering of prerequisites corresponds to an ordering of criteria regarding theory specificity. This correlation I take as further grounds for my claim that conceptual development is the development of capacities for conducting research.

In the case of mass, visibility, tangibility, etc. appear in common sense as well as all physical theories as sufficient conditions for applying the qualitative predicate '... has mass.' These conditions determine a nontechnical sense for the predicate, a sense which is as nearly identical to the sense of '... is a material object' as can be diagnosed in view of the vagaries of 'ordinary language' and commonsense. We may place the necessary and sufficient conditions '... is capable of less than maximal velocity' as adding a more technical aspect to the meaning of '... has mass,' for the addition of this property extends our understanding of mass to objects that do not satisfy conditions of tangibility, visibility, etc. Accordingly, our capacities for applying the predicate are extended to cases in which we believe with some justification, whether empirical or theoretical, that velocity is less than maximal. These capacities are shared by specialists committed to relativistic particle mechanics and by some committed to classical particle mechanics.

However, against this background, relativistic and classical physicists differ in their qualitative and quantitative conceptions of mass. The qualitative conception is significantly clarified by the assumption that maximal velocity coincides with the velocity of light, *c*. The quantitative conception is revised (though not further clarified) by the syntactical assumption relativizing mass to inertial reference frames and by new criteria regarding '+' as an operation for adding mass-values.

Historical Development of the Concept of Mass

A final test for my thesis regarding criteria and meaning change is its adequacy in explicating the historical development of the concept of mass. In particular, can my account of meaning change explicate what seems to me to be an incontrovertable feature of conceptual development, viz., its continuity? In the early stages of development of dynamical concepts, mass and forces of weight and resistance to motion were not sharply distinguished. Aristotle did subscribe to tangibility as a criterion for materiality in his choice of 'haptic' (tangible) qualities, e.g., hot, cold, wet, dry, dense, rare, rough, smooth, hard, soft as fundamental qualities of matter. However, his failure to grasp the inertial aspect of mass is evident in his construal of resistance to motion entirely as a result of interaction with the surrounding medium, and not as an intrinsic quality. Jean Buridan characterized material bodies as bearers of impetus, a disposition to continue moving until corrupted by opposing forces. The capacity for impetus depends upon one inherent attribute, the 'quantity of matter,' as well as the actual motion possessed by a material object. However, impetus is distinct from classical inertia in that it manifests itself as a cause and not an effect of motion in empty space, and hence is a force. Kepler was probably the first to combine the attributes of inherency and passivity that are shared by the classical conception of mass. His 'inertia' is manifest in the resistance of material bodies such as planets to continued motion, and this resistance depends only upon the inherent 'quantity of matter' possessed by the planet. The only remaining logically relevant feature differentiating Kepler's from Newton's quality 'mass' is the Newtonian specification that resistance to continued motion is resistance to acceleration, not velocity or rest. This specification can be construed as a revision of Kepler's criteria for '... has mass', an addition to criteria shared by Kepler and Newton whereby mass and force are distinguished, and finally an addition to criteria shared by all regarding which objects are material. Accordingly, the development of the qualitative conception of mass is incremental, though not always cumulative. The continuity is preserved by shared background criteria, but incremental specifications can be and have been withdrawn.

❑❑❑

Index

□□□

31.	A Text Book of Environmental Studies	175/-
32.	Teaching of History	175/-
33.	Administrative Thinkers	175/-
34.	Research Methodology	175/-
35.	Curriculum Development	195/-
36.	Teaching of Science	160/-
37.	Teaching of Mathematics	160/-
38.	Principles of Educational &Vocational Guidance	175/-
39.	Child Psychology	175/-
40.	Abnormal Psychology	175/-
41.	Indian Education in Emerging Society	175/-
42.	Human Resource Management	160/-
43.	Higher Education and Global Challenges	175/-
44.	Teaching of Geography	150/-
45.	Teaching of Social Studies	150/-
46.	Teaching of English	175/-
47.	Principles of Office Management (Revised Ed.)	250/-
48.	Education for All: The Indian Saga	175/-
49.	Value Education in Global Perspective	175/-
50.	Teacher Training	150/-
51.	Public Administration	150/-
52.	Public Relations & Integrated Communications	195/-
53.	Educational Psychology	150/-
54.	Introduction to Educational Technology	175/-
55.	Textbook of Food and Nutrition	150/-

Lotus PRESS

4263/3, Ansari Road,
Darya Ganj, New Delhi-110 002
Ph.: 32903912, 23280047,9811594448
E-mail: lotus_press@sify.com
www.lotuspress.co.in